D0531972

INNOCENCE and ARSENIC

A JOAN KAHN BOOK

INNOCENCE
and
ARSENIC

Studies in Crime and Literature

Albert Borowitz

HARPER & ROW, PUBLISHERS
New York, Hagerstown, San Francisco, London

Portions of this work appeared originally in *Unicorn, Nineteenth-Century French Studies, The American Scholar, The Musical Quarterly, American Bar Association Journal* and, in somewhat different form, in *The Victorian Newsletter* and *The Armchair Detective*. The translated excerpts from the Latin in Chapter Seven are by H. Grose Hodge.

FIRST EDITION

Designed by Stephanie Krasnow

Library of Congress Cataloging in Publication Data

Borowitz, Albert, 1930–
   Innocence and arsenic.
   1. Crime in literature—Addresses, essays, lectures.
   I. Title.
PN56.C7B6   809'.935'364   76-26262
ISBN 0–06–010413–9

77 78 79 80 10 9 8 7 6 5 4 3 2 1

To Fair Helen, who gave me Peter, Joan and Andrew,
In memory of my mother, and
To my father, who gave me a happy childhood in his great library

Contents

Preface

With this collection of essays on crime, I hope to make a modest contribution to a great literature which has given me pleasure since I was a child. I am very fond of the traditional detective story and pay it some tribute in these pages, particularly in the piece on *Edwin Drood*. However, in recent years my passion has been the study of factual accounts or imaginative or fictional reconstructions of true criminal cases. There is a huge body of writing in this field, including classic works of imagination by Scott, Browning and Stevenson, and impressive factual studies by William Roughead, Edmund Pearson and such talented contemporaries as Edgar Lustgarten.

I am drawn to works based on actual criminal experience because of the intriguing ambiguity of real crimes. There is uncertainty often as to guilt or innocence, and uncertainty even oftener as to the motivations of the criminal and other participants in the drama. The appeal of such literature seems to me to be just the opposite of that of the classic detective story, where all doubts and suspense are finally resolved by the ingenious detective and the evil are firmly separated from the innocent. The ambiguity of historical crime is closer to the state of constant suspense in which we live. In the detective novel the puzzle is solved at the end, but in the study of crime, as in life, the puzzle goes on forever. In the title of my collection, I adopt a famous phrase from the work of the great nineteenth-century Swedish novelist C. J. L. Almqvist. The full quotation is: "Two things are white: innocence and arsenic." There can be no better statement of the ambiguity of criminal conduct, or any other human conduct, for that matter.

As I planned the essays, I decided to stake out a special area of the crime field for my writing. Having great interest in literature and music, I decided to concentrate on cases in which writers or musicians are brought into direct confrontation with crime (as participants in criminal cases or trials, as spectators of crime or punishment, or as the subjects of murder legends), and on crimes that provide the basis for significant literary works. In addition, because I like to study foreign languages and cultures, I chose material from many countries and periods rather than limiting myself to Britain and America, as many of my predecessors have done. I hoped to communicate my enthusiasm for the varied social settings of crimes, for nothing can show better how people live than the strange circumstances under which they are sometimes done to death.

"The Snows on the Moors," a discussion of the writings of C. P. Snow and Pamela Hansford Johnson on the Moors murder case, stands as a general introduction to my views on the literature of crime and punishment. I hope that it may help illumine some of the other studies which follow.

Many great writers about crime have had unusually strong powers to see themselves in the criminals' place. The identification by Robert Louis Stevenson of elements of his personality with the impulses of Mr. Hyde combined with Stevenson's knowledge of British criminal history to produce his great tale, which is discussed in "Dr. Jekyll and Mr. Stevenson." Just as Stevenson could identify himself with a murderer, so Thackeray felt strong empathy with a hanged man. The chapter "Why Thackeray Went to See a Man Hanged" shows a writer in one of his most attractive relations to crime, as spokesman for the public conscience. Thackeray was, like most of his contemporaries, fascinated with crime and criminal history, and even felt in himself a certain morbid interest in public hanging. But when he went to see a man hanged, he found that his flesh and personality were revolted and out of his experience produced an eloquent and uniquely personal protest against capital punishment.

Dickens's attraction to the exploration of the criminal mind increased in his late works and became remarkably intense in *The Mystery of Edwin Drood*, his unfinished novel. In the article on the *Drood* fragment, I note the range of detective-story techniques which Dickens would have had at his disposal in arriving at a solution of the mystery. The debates about the ending of *Drood* will doubtless go on forever, but Dickens's work went far enough to establish one point beyond dispute: that in a detective-story format, important social issues can be grappled with and a major piece of literature can result.

The possible coexistence of genius and criminality is an intriguing subject. Criminal history does not record many portraits of creative geniuses as murderers. We have the crimes of the composer Gesualdo and the painter Caravaggio, but they were crimes of passion committed in the violent setting of Renaissance and seventeenth-century Italy. It is true that in 1679 Jean Racine, the great French dramatist, was accused of poisoning his mistress, the actress Mlle. Duparc, and of stealing a valuable diamond from her finger while she lay on her deathbed. But nobody took this charge too seriously, since Racine's accuser, La Voisin, was herself one of the leading poisoners of the time. And even if Racine was guilty, he had done no more than succumb to the bad habits of his age, when arsenic was used so routinely to pass riches from hand to hand that it became known as "inheritance powder."

The article on the legend of the murder of Mozart by

Salieri presents musicians in the roles of murderer and victim. One of the comforts of the classic detective story is that we never much care about the murder victims who are regularly disposed of at the vicarage or on the train. However, history does not spare our feelings and gives us many painful examples of beloved geniuses who were murdered or, as in Mozart's case, seriously thought to have been murdered. I was particularly attracted to the Mozart murder legend, not only by my love for Mozart and his music, but because the legend gave rise to one of the great literary works exploring the relation between genius and criminality, Pushkin's play *Mozart and Salieri.*

In "New Gaslight on Jack the Ripper" I have poked good-natured fun at writers assuming a role in crime for which they are usually poorly suited, that of armchair detectives. I am not much impressed with the new theories attempting to establish Jack's identity, and I have even emerged with a certain sympathy for Jack, pursued as he is after a century by a host of self-appointed sleuths. So here is a toast to you, Jack, from the twentieth century. We're killing more now, but enjoying it less.

In the article on Cicero's defense of Cluentius, I deal with a brilliant writer participating directly in a criminal trial as defense counsel. In Cicero's day there was no distinction between law and literature. Although Cicero's speeches, including the defense of Cluentius, were undoubtedly polished and elaborated at leisure when the trials were over, both Cicero's oral presentation to the jury and the carefully crafted orations he has left us were based on the principles of rhetoric. Rhetoric had a single purpose: not to mirror objective truth, but to persuade. Initially Cicero sought to persuade the jury, and ever after he has been presenting his arguments to posterity. I do not know, therefore, whether Cicero's picture of the crimes of Cluentius's prosecutors should be classified as fact or fiction. It is probably to a great extent a product of Cicero's rhetorical imagination.

The case of Aldo Braibanti concerns a writer as criminal defendant, facing a charge of "psychological kidnapping" of two young men. In Braibanti's trial, as in the Sacco and Vanzetti case, the defendant's leftist writings were put in evidence. His essays were considered as competent to show how he might have exercised undue influence on two unsophisticated youths. It is a disturbing assumption of the Braibanti case that the tie between literature and conduct can be proved to the satisfaction of a jury in a criminal court. More broadly, the Braibanti case raises a legal question which has recently become of great interest in connection with the trial of Patty Hearst, namely, the extent to which concepts like "brainwashing" can be effectively defined and determined by traditional criminal procedures.

The Braibanti article, which was originally published in *The American Bar Association Journal,* has given me some special rewards. First, the term "psychological kidnapping," which I coined as a free translation of the Italian crime with which Braibanti was charged, has now passed into common journalistic use. Furthermore, the article has aroused interest among individuals and groups who stand in opposite positions on the issues raised by the case, including on the one hand parents and prosecutors concerned with the loss of children to proselytizing cults, and on the other, professionals who oppose the use of psychiatric confinement or reconditioning of wayward citizens or children by repressive governments or parents.

In the study of Latouche and Clarisse Manson, I write about the famous Fualdès murder case, in early-nineteenth-century France, which inspired a series of drawings by Géricault. Here there is a curious double interaction between fact and fiction. In the course of the trials of Fualdès's accused murderers, the principal witness, Clarisse Manson, who may have been a pathological liar, turned her unreliable trial testimony into a memoir. Her book was written in collaboration with the journalist and man of letters Henri de

Latouche, who apparently shared her difficulty in separating fact from imagination.

In "The Jackal and I, or How to Do Research in London," I tell all my professional secrets about how I go about gathering material for my articles on English crime. In view of the problems I encountered (which are amusing only in retrospect), the article can hardly be regarded as inspirational to other writers who are interested in the crime field, but it has the merit of being true.

Before I leave you to my writings, with the hope that you will find them of interest, I would like to greet you with a motto that is most fitting for any study of sudden death:

To life!

Albert Borowitz

Cleveland, Ohio
1976

INNOCENCE and ARSENIC

CHAPTER ONE

The Snows on the Moors

C. P. Snow and Pamela Hansford Johnson
on the Moors Murder Case

Husbands and wives have been known to hold strong views about many things, and marriage provides no guarantee that those views will be congruent. Although popular fiction and cinema have attempted to present as intrinsically interesting the variances between husband's and wife's assessments of the same facts and events, there is perhaps in general no more reason to collect opinions in the "his" and "hers" versions than the towels, sleeping ensembles or other commodities that are customarily marketed in the same manner. When the husband and wife in question are novelists as distinguished as C. P. Snow and Pamela Hansford Johnson, however, and the object of their views is one of the most disturbing murder trials of our day, the Moors Murder Trial, a comparison of their individual attitudes may illustrate the possibility of highly personal intellectual and emotional responses by two thinkers bound by marriage, and at the same time assist the continuing assessment and development of public views on a matter of human and social concern.

Pamela Hansford Johnson's reflections on the trial of Ian Brady and Myra Hindley, the so-called Moors Murder Trial, were published in her essay *On Iniquity: Some Personal Reflections Arising Out of the Moors Murder Trial* (1967). C. P. Snow used the Moors Trial as the basis for the next-to-last novel in the *Strangers and Brothers* cycle, *The Sleep of Reason* (1968). Despite the fact that the *Strangers and Brothers* series is rooted in actual events of modern history, it can, of course, be misleading to take *The Sleep of Reason* to be a literal retelling of the Moors Trial. Just as its immediate predecessor, *The Corridors of Power*, carries strong overtones of the Profumo affair, while stirring fainter reminiscences of the Dilke scandal, so *The Sleep of Reason* reminds us not only of Brady and Hindley, but also of the trial of the girls Parker and Hulme in New Zealand, and ultimately of the Loeb and Leopold case.

C. P. Snow's treatment of crime in *The Sleep of Reason* takes on added interest in light of the relatively recent paperback publication of his early detective novel, *Death Under Sail*, which first appeared in 1932. Although Snow now dismisses *Death Under Sail* as "a stylised, artificial detective story very much in the manner of the day," it has sufficient formal and thematic links with his mature work to warrant our noting, although with a light hand, the continuity of certain of Snow's thoughts about murder and crime. Even the most superficial glance at *Death Under Sail* immediately renews our acquaintance with the formal signposts marking the mature novels: the short, provocative chapter headings, and the habit of ending a chapter with one character addressing an intriguing question or Delphic pronouncement to an unprepared companion. The narrative raw materials also bear a family resemblance to those of the later works. We see in the early Snow whodunit the prominent use of a theme that was to run through many of the *Strangers and Brothers* books—the significance of integrity in scientific research as a touchstone of character and reaction in crisis.

A shared assumption underlies *On Iniquity* and *The Sleep of Reason:* that a crime or criminal trial may merit the close scrutiny of an intelligent person not professionally concerned with law or criminology. The question of why this should be so, although not capable of definitive answer, is a fascinating one and has received a good deal of attention in the literature of crime. Many of the alternative views are recorded by Patricia Pitman and Colin Wilson in their respective introductions to their joint work, *Encyclopedia of Murder* (1962). Colin Wilson, in his preface, entitled "The Study of Murder," accounts for his interest in murder by relating the subject to his "outsider" thesis. He conceives the possibility of viewing an encyclopedia of murder as a series of exhibits in a lecture on the meaning of existentialism, in which one can ask each murderer his estimate of the value of life, "and get from him the answer in quite precise physical terms: ten pounds, a snub, my wife's infidelity, a broken engagement, etc."

In *A Casebook of Murder* (1969), Wilson elaborated the basis of his interest in crime, which he characterized as "philosophical." To him, the interesting thing about the Moors murderers, Brady and Hindley, "is that they were responding to certain social pressures with *freedom of choice.*" He makes more specific his identification of the murderer with the "outsider," in a manner that is surprisingly flattering to the murdering classes. He finds that society produces a substratum of five percent consisting of alienated men of often considerable imagination who feel resentment toward society and who are faced with obstacles, the overcoming of which may lead to art and creativity or to crime. The theoretical roots of this view are weakened a bit by Wilson's candid revelation that he regards abstract artists and atonal composers as little more than criminals whom society permits to run at large.

In asserting that philosophy is the proper ground for an interest in crime, Wilson expressly rejects the "aesthetic" approach to crime writing that derived from Thomas De Quincey and was adopted by those modern masters among British and American crime writers William Roughead and Edmund Pearson. This school of writing, by ironic reference to standards determining the "beauty" of great crimes and by telling of murder in a predominantly humorous style, makes itself an easy target for Wilson's charge that such writers take unfeeling pleasure in human tragedy. In Snow's Inspector Birrell in *Death Under Sail,* we have a good-natured caricature of the crime aesthetician, with his flatulent insistence that murder, like any other art, is determined by its "tempo." The classic crime writers, however, may be understood as claiming quite simply that crime is significant as drama, independent of philosophical or sociological implications. And if we include in this concept of drama the light that crimes may shed on social milieus and living patterns, we may list among the adherents of the "murder for aesthetics" school rejected by Wilson some very improbable literary aficionados of "true crime." One such enthusiast was Henry James, who, in encouraging Roughead to return from witch stories to crime writing, wrote him that he should "go back to the dear old human and sociable murders and adulteries and forgeries in which we are so agreeably at home."

It is possible to understand Wilson's distaste for the traditional crime writers in terms quite different from the dichotomy he offers between the "philosophical" and "aesthetic" approaches to a horrifying subject. Underlying his sense of a relationship between the criminal and the creative "outsider" appears to be a belief that the ideal crime writer should identify himself to a high degree with the criminal. Patricia Pitman, in her preface to her joint work with Wilson, takes a diametrically opposed view. She notes that the view that we are all murderers under the skin is "certainly a fashionable view." It is Miss Pitman's opinion, however, fortified by her reading of the very writers whom Wilson rejects, that: "We are fascinated by murderers not because they are so like the rest of us but because they are so utterly different. I believe that most people are born with an instinct against cold-blooded killing and that murderers lack this instinct."

C. P. Snow and Pamela Hansford Johnson in their treatments of the Moors Trial obviously share the assumption made by both Wilson and Pitman that the conduct of the criminal has a significant relationship with the observer's view of his own conduct and choices. But both Snow and Johnson appear to emphasize, as does Pitman, the observer's differentiation of himself from the criminal rather than the identification that appears inherent in Wilson's "philosophical" approach. And unlike Wilson, who sees murderers as related to creative outsiders, Snow and Johnson are concerned with the impact of crime upon the normal life of a community of observers.

The reference to the disreputable concept of the normal life may be forgiven in this context. For it appears clear that to both C. P. Snow and Pamela Hansford Johnson the phenomenon of crime has significance not only in itself, but also as a surrogate for the larger disasters that befall mankind. When one turns one's attention from war or genocide to the study of a criminal case, even one as brutal as the Moors murders, there is perhaps some unconfessed comfort in the scaling down of the losses, and the consideration in retrospect of what might have been done to avert the tragedy.

In this sense there is substance in the enthusiasm that the study of murder inspires in Inspector Birrell, the humorous crime buff in *Death Under Sail*. With the experience of World War II still lying ahead, Birrell refers to the investigation of crime as "one of the greatest romances in the world" and "a sign of all the good in our modern world." He rejoices that detective stories have replaced "ballads about war and brute force and lust."

In Snow's *The Sleep of Reason*, Lewis Eliot's thoughts about the murder trial evoke memories of films of Auschwitz. Lewis Eliot admits to feeling a "shameful and disgusting pleasure" while watching the films—a fascination "because men could do these things to other men." But the crucial point is that this fascination with Auschwitz, with the cruelty of man to man, does not overbear in either Snow's work or

Johnson's the faith in the "normal" life, nor does it relieve or limit the responsibilities of that life. It is clear that neither writer is afflicted by what might be called the "Auschwitz syndrome," or the "Hiroshima syndrome": the tendency of many contemporary writers to excuse individual failures of morality or responsibility by setting them against a backdrop of the cruelties of modern history. American literature and drama since World War II have given us no more illuminating example of the Auschwitz syndrome than Arthur Miller's play *After the Fall*, which opens its action against the silhouetted towers of a German concentration camp and proceeds to justify Quentin's failures in his relationships with his wife, Maggie, and others with the question: "Who can be innocent again on this mountain of skulls?"

Neither Snow nor Johnson returns from the view of crime or disaster with such a palliative for private standards of conduct. In *The Sleep of Reason*, Martin Eliot has little use for the easy switching on of the Auschwitz syndrome. He has contempt for a journalist whose articles on the trial will likely take the "all men are murderers" tack: "Great throbbing pieces about how we're all guilty. So really no one is guilty. So really everything is as well as could be expected in an admittedly imperfect world." Miss Johnson's view is put even more directly: "The murder of one single child is made negligible by *nothing*, not even by Hiroshima."

Pamela Hansford Johnson was asked by the *Sunday Telegraph* "to spend a day or so at the Moors Trial and write of [her] impressions." But the effect of the trial was so strong that she wrote her book *On Iniquity* to discuss at length the "social implications" of the case.

The facts of the Moors case are so horrifying that it is a relief to be able to present them very briefly on the ground of their general notoriety. Ian Brady, aged twenty-seven, and his mistress, Myra Hindley, aged twenty-three, were charged with the murder of a seventeen-year-old youth, Edward Evans, and of two preadolescent children, Lesley Ann Downey and John Kilbride. (More specifically, Brady was charged with the murder of all three victims. Hindley was charged with the murder of Evans and Downey and of harboring Brady in connection with his murder of Kilbride.) The trial derived its sobriquet from the fact that the victims' bodies were discovered buried on the moors near Manchester. All the murders were brutal and preceded by sexual assault or by torture. The interest of the murderers in de Sade, torture and Nazism was documented by Brady's collection of books, which he bundled into suitcases and checked at a parcel room at Manchester Central Station prior to the last murder. The sufferings of little Lesley Downey and her pleas for mercy were recorded by the murderers on a tape stored with their pornography collection, and they had also recorded their questioning of a friend of Lesley's with respect to the missing girl.

Early in the case, Brady admitted the murder of Evans, and the line of defense on this charge appeared to be an attempt to prove lack of premeditation so as to mitigate punishment. On all other charges Brady and Hindley pleaded not guilty. Because of the defenses taken, the sanity of the defendants was not in issue, and the trial, with a total absence of psychiatric testimony, frustrated the desire of observers for some professional insights into the murderers' characters. It is observed in John Deane Potter's *The Monsters of the Moors* (1966) that the discovery of the crimes occurred about the same time as the passing of the 1965 No Hanging Bill. Mr. Potter speculates that if the crimes had remained capital, the introduction of psychiatric evidence in support of a plea of insanity would have been much more likely.

The accused were found guilty on all counts, and were sentenced to life imprisonment.

There is no doubt that Pamela Hansford Johnson's attendance at the Moors Trial drew heavily on her emotional reserves. It may not be fanciful to find a reflection of C. P.

Snow's concern over the profound effect of the trial on his wife in Lewis Eliot's comments on his wife Margaret's reaction to the trial of the young murderesses in *The Sleep of Reason.* He says that Margaret "had believed that she would be stronger than I was," but was "appalled" by her first day in court. Without doubting in the slightest the reality of the experiences Miss Johnson recounts, the reader of *On Iniquity* must be promptly struck by the degree to which, even prior to her first attendance at the Moors Trial, Miss Johnson found the town of Chester, where the trial was held, to be permeated by the evil that she was to find emanating from the case. She recalls her shock at noting that a couple of lovers, when breaking off their embrace in a public place, revealed themselves to be two males. She goes on to tell us how her walk through the town was ruined by her observation that she was being followed by an elderly man—ruined despite a feminine calculation that the old fellow was quite harmless. At the trial a silent relationship appeared to establish itself between her and the accused murderess—Myra Hindley seemed to look at her with hatred.

Although these impressions of pervasive evil are subjective in the extreme, they serve to dramatize Miss Johnson's thesis that there are evil people whose actions cannot be explained away as "sickness," and that Brady and Hindley were evil. It is significant that a writer as sophisticated as Miss Johnson shares with the popular journalists the feeling that the two murderers are most aptly described as monsters.

Regarding the murderers as evil, Miss Johnson then faces the problem of relating the criminals' natures to her conception of her own. She refuses to manufacture a false empathy with Hindley, although she recognizes a general element of violence in the pleasure derived by many adults (including herself) in disciplining unruly children. (It is interesting to note that in *The Sleep of Reason* one of the murderesses, in her confession, recreated the dynamics of the crime in terms of the pretended parental discipline of the child victim.) Miss

Johnson, however, does not believe that she could have committed the Moors crime; she says that her "instincts do not lie in the direction of Hindley's."

Finding iniquity in the Moors murderers, Miss Johnson devotes the bulk of her study to an inquiry into whether society has contributed to the breakdown of the murderers' inhibitions and the release of their wickedness into action. She answers this question in the affirmative, placing the blame on an all-permissive society that has given the masses freedom to indulge in violence and pornography, has encouraged the desire for instant self-gratification, and has given rise to a blunting of the sensibilities, which Miss Johnson likes to call *affectlessness*.

In view of the quite literal involvement of the murderers' minds in Nazism, it may be too easy to cite Miss Johnson's essay in support of the thesis that the study of crime has a logical and psychological tie with concern for the larger human cruelties and disasters. Nevertheless, it is striking how often the case in Miss Johnson's eyes summons up visions of Nazi Germany. She can visualize Myra Hindley as an affectless concentration camp guard. And as the trial in *The Sleep of Reason* had reminded Lewis Eliot of a film of Auschwitz he had seen, so Miss Johnson is reminded of a viewing of films of the overrunning of Belsen.

The attack on the affectless society in *On Iniquity*, however, turns out to be the prelude to what appears to be a primary concern with pornography and the portrayal of violence in literary and dramatic form, and a plea for the continuation of censorship. This aspect of the essay appears to reflect highly personal views of the author, which may have been strongly held prior to the Moors Trial although they were reinforced by what Miss Johnson saw there. There is, for example, that English prejudice, which appeared in the Trial of Lady Chatterley, against permitting pornography to come into the hands of the lower classes. I call it a prejudice, because even if it be assumed that pornography may incite to crime, the study of criminal history will not show that multiple lust killings are the peculiar preserve of the lower classes. In any event, Miss Johnson is candid in recalling in her essay that she had a little earlier stirred controversy by suggesting that Krafft-Ebing's work should not be made available in a paperback edition.

Another personal aspect of Miss Johnson's assault on pornography is a failure to distinguish between eroticism and the display of violence. One gets the impression that the archvillains of permissiveness are to her the people who freed *Lady Chatterley* for mass adoration, and she notes as an immediate consequence of the *Lady Chatterley* trial that young people felt compelled to use four-letter words on the street.

The focus of Miss Johnson's analysis on the single element of pornography is surprising in the light of her rejection as simplistic of an explanation of Brady's criminal development on the sole ground of his illegitimacy. Moreover, even if the principal object of Miss Johnson's attack be taken to be the portrayal of violence, the facts of the Moors Trial will not bear her out. Miss Johnson cannot very well argue that Brady was initially corrupted by his reading, since in his childhood he engaged in the sadistic killing of animals. Can his proclivities have been aggravated by his reading? Although Brady's library included many works on torture, who is to say that he was more aroused and influenced by them than by his reading of *Mein Kampf* and his other books on Nazism? Even if we could rally our forces against literary violence, who will answer the call if we seek to repeal the violence of recent history? Miss Johnson herself marshals against her own argument the possibility that one of the most fiendish touches of the murderers' torture of the Downey girl, the playing of Christmas music as background for the recording of her screams, may have been influenced by a scene in the serious war movie *The Victors*, where an execution was performed against a background of Christmas music. (It may also be noted that the cult of Charles Manson drew its ideological sustenance from such disparate sources as Robert Heinlein's science fiction work *Stranger in a Strange Land,* a Beatles song, "Helter Skelter," and the book of Revelation in the Bible.)

The affectlessness of Brady and Hindley is no doubt the keynote of the case. But in Miss Johnson's concentration on pornography and its role in the crimes, she may have neglected evidence of other methods of destruction of the murderers' inhibitions that have "social implications." For example, it is reported by John Deane Potter that Brady brought himself to the proper pitch for criminal activity by taking "pep" pills. But the role of drugs in the case is not mentioned by Miss Johnson. Moreover, one cannot help but be struck by the role of technological recording media in the case—the recording of torture on tape, the pornographic photographs of the Downey girl under constraint, and the photographs of Hindley taken at the site of the graves on the moors. There is a suggestion in the case that the murderers had such a weak sense of their own reality and the reality of their horrible actions that only the use of recording media could provide them with sufficient evidence of who they were and what they had accomplished. The supplanting of individual perception and feeling by the images of the media has, of course, been the subject of some of our most interesting contemporary films and plays, including *Blow-Up, Medium Cool, We Bombed in New Haven* and the charming musical *The Last Sweet Days of Isaac.*

The preoccupation of Brady and Hindley with recording themselves becomes the focal point of a black-comedy variation on the Moors case theme, David Halliwell's play *K. D. Dufford hears K. D. Dufford ask K. D. Dufford how K. D. Dufford'll make K. D. Dufford* (1970). In Dufford, the murderer, there is a high degree of suspicion, of worry about the impression he is making on others, but no sense of his own reality. His prime concern is for his "image," and as Mrs.

Shamefoot's ambition in Ronald Firbank's *Vainglory* was to become a stained-glass window, so Dufford's dream is to become, through his self-photographed murder, an image on film and, he hopes, a lead article in a newspaper. The play provides many versions of the murder scene, and the most successful captures the recording fantasies of the Moors murderers by having the child victim photographing her bumbling attackers. Dufford achieves his ambitions to an extent beyond his wildest expectations. The crime inspires a spate of commentaries in all the media. The last is a book (distressingly by an American) that enthusiastically reflects Dufford's concern for recording and propagating his criminal acts by its title, "DUFFORD A Study of Murder as Public Relations." Ironically, Dufford himself does not recognize his kinship with the photophiliac Brady. Reading of the Moors case, Dufford remarks, "probably just sex."

Dufford is at the end destined to become a popular song, a song that, in doggerel, neatly sidesteps the issue of whether the public identifies with murderers or differentiates itself from them:

> And yet Keith Dufford was a man
> Who walked on two legs, had no tail,
> Who must have seen the sun and felt the rain.
> Oh how was he diff'rent, how was he diff'rent,
> and how am I the same?

It has been justly observed that Emlyn Williams's *Beyond Belief* (1967), which fleshes out a factual account of the Moors case with the author's fictional "surmises," shares with Miss Johnson's work an emphasis on the murderers' readings in sadism and the prevalence of portrayed violence. The place of cinematic violence in the atmosphere in which Brady and Hindley grew up is marked by continual quotations of lurid titles from movie marquees. But Williams, to a greater extent than Miss Johnson, is concerned about the impact of the pornography of historic violence. In fact, he theorizes that the murder of John Kilbride may have been suggested by the murder of President Kennedy the day before. Beyond this reference to the aura of violence, Williams portrays the crime, in rather traditional terms, as growing from the roots of childhood experiences and from the poor quality of urban life. Ultimately, however, he pauses before the "mysteries of identity . . . the spells which are woven after birth, the subtle processes working from day to day in the darkness of the young head, as it grows from childhood to adolescence and maturity."

It should not surprise us that Miss Johnson, who is, after all, a novelist by trade, should, despite the social message of *On Iniquity*, stand in awe before the mystery of the personal relationship between Brady and Hindley. She finds the case to be "a touchstone of what can go hideously wrong with two people." In dealing with their development into criminals, she has recourse to the psychiatric concept that is a favorite of amateur criminologists, *folie à deux*. In the hands of the amateurs this concept becomes a notion that two individuals who separately might have stayed within the bounds of conduct that society tolerates may, by interaction with each other's personalities and fantasies, drive themselves into the abyss of criminality.

Although the state of *folie à deux* is recognized by professional psychiatrists, it appears that the amateurs of crime have a more romantic theorem than the good doctors would accept—that the combination of fantasies of partners locked in *folie à deux* is so unusual that neither partner would have been likely to find another partnership with the same lethal consequences. It may therefore be that the amateur concept of *folie à deux* is the infernal parallel of the belief that marriages are made in heaven.

Miss Johnson is tempted to determine that one of the murderers was the dominant partner in the psychological deterioration of the couple, and she eventually fixes upon Brady. "He read, he led, she followed," Miss Johnson writes. The accuracy of labeling either party as fully dominant, however, is put in question by Miss Johnson's feeling early in the trial that Myra Hindley was the motive force behind her lover. No one-sided view of the relationship appears satisfying after a review of the evidence. A striking point is that Hindley, whom Miss Johnson finally tabs as subservient, did all the driving in the pair's criminal expeditions and that Brady apparently never obtained a driver's license. It may be that Miss Johnson, misled by her emphasis on pornography, formed the impression that Brady, who seemed to have the deeper interest in pornography and had a long involvement in sadism, was therefore more "abnormal" than Hindley. Miss Johnson, however, ignores the suggestions of abnormality in Hindley. Myra Hindley posed for pornographic photographs with her dog, and her most violent display of emotion in the entire case was upon being informed of the death of her dog in the course of police laboratory tests to determine his age.

Miss Johnson also displays the penchant of crime writers since F. Tennyson Jesse for classifying crimes, much in the manner that Polonius classified plays in *Hamlet*. She places the Moors crimes in the category of "the corporate murder, by two or more people of two or more people." On the basis of the number of victims, she distinguishes the case from that of Loeb and Leopold and suggests a similarity to the activities of medieval covens. The number of victims, however, is a very unsatisfactory way of categorizing crimes, and a student of the Loeb-Leopold case might be content to attribute the nonrepetition of the murder to quick detective work (or to the loss of Leopold's glasses, if one prefers) rather than to a fulfillment of the criminal impulse. If the subclassification "corporate murder" is helpful, I would prefer a distinction based on the choice of victim: was he selected at random or was he the subject of special hostility on the part of one or more of the murdering group? It is the pure chance of selection of the victim that places the Moors case closer to Loeb-

Leopold than to such cases as that of Pauline Parker and Juliet Hulme, who murdered Pauline's mother because she was attempting to end their relationship, or those of the traditional corporate murderers of the unwanted husband, such as Edith Thompson and Frederick Bywaters, Ruth Snyder and Judd Gray, and the like. The comparison of the corporate murders of multiple victims to medieval witcheries may be comforting by the distance that the allusion lends, and Miss Johnson states that they are rare in the nineteenth and twentieth centuries. Such crimes, however, are unfortunately very much a part of the modern scene. We may recall as an example the murderous automobile journey of Charles Starkweather and his girl friend. And Miss Johnson's description of the role of the charismatic leader in corporate murders reads chillingly like a prescient vision of the Manson cult.

At the end of the essay Miss Johnson returns again to her quarrel with pornography, which she expands to cosmic scope. In raising the question of whether the Moors case would not justify a restriction of literary freedom, she stands Dostoevsky on his head. Ivan Karamazov, because of the suffering of children and the "other tears of humanity with which the earth is soaked from its crust to its centre," is anxious to return to God his entrance ticket to life. He declares that the "higher harmony" in which the religious Alyosha believes is "not worth the tears of . . . one tortured child." Miss Johnson writes that she is unwilling to return her ticket, even after having seen the film of Belsen and even after the Moors case. Instead she suggests, without deciding, that broad restriction of literary freedom may be worthwhile if it can prevent the suffering of a single child. She cannot accept the notion that evil and cruelty are a necessary imperfection of humanity. Instead of finding the tears of a single child the basis for rejecting a religious concept of life, she would consider altering the living and cultural patterns of millions if the possible result may be to spare that child. Of such emotional and intellectual stuff are both generous spirits and extremists born.

In determining to insert a crime resembling the Moors case into his *roman fleuve,* C. P. Snow was able to select from a number of alternative methods of relating the trial to the lives of the principal characters: the use of the trial as a public event in which the characters would express and develop views purely in the roles of citizens (a fictional parallel of Pamela Hansford Johnson's work); the introduction of a character into the processes of the trial in a professional capacity; or the establishment of a personal relationship between the principal characters and the participants in the crime. Snow elected to make one of the accused murderesses, Cora Ross, a niece of Lewis Eliot's childhood friend George Passant. She and Kitty Pateman, with whom she is having a love affair, are accused of torturing and murdering an eight-year-old child. Snow's decision to establish a personal tie with one of the murderesses does not appear to have been made for technical considerations alone. The close relation between the observers and the trial is very much in keeping with the point of view from which events are generally seen in Snow's fiction. Despite the fact that C. P. Snow, the novelist, is also Lord Snow, the scientist and public servant, he is primarily concerned in his fiction with personal and social relations within relatively small groups, and the impact of the outside world and of contemporary history is recorded in reactions and interreactions of the group members. Snow's early *Death Under Sail,* which describes the murder of a host at a boating party and the reactions of the guests while in seclusion at a cottage after the crime, obviously resembles the Agatha Christie "murder at the priory" school, but ironically also looks forward to the group emphasis of Snow's mature novels.

The application of this method to the contemplation of the crime in *The Sleep of Reason* does impose some limitation on the scope of Snow's insights. The brutal crime is "domesticated" by bringing its perpetrator within the family group of the novel. As a consequence, the fundamental question with which the novel and many serious crime books must grapple, the significance of a crime to the outside observer, is oversimplified from the start: Lewis Eliot *must* contemplate the crime and come to grips with it because it involves a relative of his close friend.

At the same time, the observation of the crime through the eyes of a related group has an organic relation to a basic tenet of the *Strangers and Brothers* series: that the "flow" of life through the channels of career, marriage, friendship and group relations is the normal source of happiness and satisfaction, and that the disasters of illness, loss of loved ones, war, scandal and crime are diversions of this "flow." These diversions are, one hopes, temporary, but, to quote the Sophoclean dictum of Lewis Eliot in *The Sleep of Reason,* "Call no man happy until he is dead." The notion of the diversions of the flow of life is referred to by Snow in *The Sleep of Reason* as "arrests of life." He explicitly pairs as examples of such "arrests" Lewis Eliot's suffering from a detached retina and the impact on him and his friends of the trial of George Passant's niece. Moreover, the relation of crime with war and genocide as disruptions of ordinary life is continually stressed by the characters' recollections of Nazi concentration camps. Snow's vision of Auschwitz, however, does not overbear his confidence in the values and duties of normal life. In fact, Eliot's most striking comparison of the child-murder with Auschwitz is not a view into the horrors of the prison camp but a look cast outward from the camp. He quotes the observation of a former prisoner that at Auschwitz one could not escape a degrading and ironic sense of the relativity of time—the feeling that "on the same day, *at the same moment,* people had been sitting down to meals or begetting children while, a few hundred yards away, others had been dying in torture. It had been the same with this boy's death." At the end of the novel Snow asserts the resumption of the normal flow of life in a very unassuming way, by the announcement to Lewis Eliot of his nephew's engagement.

This is not to say that either Snow or his characters take the torture and murder of a child lightly. But he perhaps is less willing than Miss Johnson to draw detailed "social implications." Lewis Eliot is not appalled by the sexual revolution. He comments that sexual freedom represents a victory of the ideas that George Passant had preached all his life, and that most people he knew did not regard fornication as an offense. Moreover, Eliot is not convinced that the new generation has fundamentally changed. Strolling across his university campus, he notes that the students, despite new clothing and social and sexual customs, still appear to be worrying about exams.

Significantly, there appears to be a deliberate discounting of specific influences of ideology or literature on the murder. Eliot is most concerned about the effect of the case on George Passant because he fears that the prosecutors (and the community) will blame Cora Ross's participation in the murder on her having belonged to the group of young people to whom her uncle had preached individual liberty and free love.

In his opening address to the jury, however, the senior counsel for the prosecution makes only a brief mention of George's group. Matthew Gough, one of the prosecution's psychiatric experts, testifies about the possible effect of the Passant group on Cora Ross. He indulges in a speculation that is surprisingly the reverse of what one often hears from the pro-censorship forces—that had Cora been less timid or inhibited, the group might have liberated her, but that "it was hurtful to live in a Venusberg without taking part oneself." Martin Eliot wonders, in a conversation with his brother Lewis, whether the crime might never have been committed if it had not been for the "hothouse air" that surrounded George and his group. Lewis Eliot's reply seems to speak for

Snow in rejecting the possibility of identifying specific ideological influences as the sources of a criminal act:

Was there ever any single cause of any action, particularly of action
such as this? Yes, they must have been affected by the atmosphere
around them, yes, they were more likely to go to the extreme in
their sexual tastes. Perhaps it made it easier for them to share their
fantasies. But between those fantasies, and what they had done,
there was still the unimaginable gap. Of course, there were influences in the air. But only people like them, predisposed to commit
sadistic horrors, anyway, would have played on to the lethal end. If
they had not had these influences, there would have been others.

Compared with Brady's testimony about his readings in
sadism, the testimony of the murderesses in *The Sleep of
Reason* about their reading habits is a distinct letdown for
the censors. Asked about what she read, Cora Ross answers
that she read nothing. Kitty Pateman, who is the reader of
the two, testified that she read Camus, but Lewis Eliot does
not believe her, thinking that she is trying to impress.

The emphatic refusal by Snow in *The Sleep of Reason* to
attribute a baleful influence to literature is in marked contrast to his position in his 1959 Rede Lecture, which was
published as *The Two Cultures and the Scientific Revolution.*
In *The Two Cultures,* Snow, in support of his preference for
the scientific over the literary "culture," quoted with approval the observation of a "scientist of distinction" that the
influence of most of the dominant writers before World War
II had brought "Auschwitz that much nearer." Strangely
enough, it is now Pamela Hansford Johnson who, in *On Iniquity,* sees a resemblance between the literature in our book-
stores and that available in the last days of the Weimar Republic, while Snow, in his novel, discounts the possibility of
corruption by literature.

In *Death Under Sail* the detective, Finbow, maintains the
primacy of psychological evidence over material facts. It appears that Snow found an incompleteness in the Moors Trial
because of the absence of psychiatric witnesses. Moreover, to

the observer of a crime who seeks to "differentiate" himself from the murderers despite his recognition of his own impulses toward violence and unreason, it is soothing to suggest that the explanation of the criminal act may, after all, be "medical." It surely must have been a relief to Ian Capel and his friends in *Death Under Sail* to discover, as we learn at the end of that novel, that the murder of their host by a member of their close social circle may have been due to the mental deterioration of the murderer as a result of a terminal disease.

In any event, considerable space is given in the recounting of the trial in *The Sleep of Reason* to presentation of evidence on the psychiatric history of the two murderesses. No individual analysis of the girls' personalities and criminal motivation is presented as completely satisfying, and Lewis Eliot is impressed by the moderation shown by all the experts in giving their views. Like Miss Johnson in her essay, Snow's prosecution witness, Dr. Cornford, favors the theory of *folie à deux* and finds that one of the killers (Cora Ross) played a dominant role in the relationship. Most of the trial observers agree with Cornford. Snow, however, through the opinions of Justice Fane and the observations of Lewis Eliot himself, holds open the possibility that the relation between the two girls may have been structured on the basis of complementary qualities rather than simplistic masculinity and femininity or dominance and submissiveness. Justice Fane is struck by Cora Ross's loyalty to Kitty Pateman. He does not think that Cora was "so much in charge" and suspects that "the little one [Kitty] is a fiend out of hell." During Eliot's visit to Cora in prison after the trial, he is struck by her habit of making all her future plans in terms of her life with Kitty, while he has little doubt that Kitty could remake her life alone. His most profound impression is that Kitty is the more imaginative of the two, and she seems to him to be a pathological liar.

Both the crime and its aftermath afford Snow an opportunity to elicit from the varied personages of *The Sleep of*

Reason a full spectrum of responses to the significance of the case and to the larger-scale human cruelties it recalls. The Gearys, a very happily married couple, are capable of regarding the crime as an "accident." To old Justice Fane, the crime provides no reason to lose his confidence in free will. He regards the murderers as responsible for their actions just as he is for his own in deciding whether to order a second gin and tonic. Both Martin Eliot, Lewis's brother, and Lewis's son, Charles, suggest, from different ideological grounds, that the particular case would not have meant as much to Lewis in the absence of his personal connections with the case. Martin's view is that of a pessimistic lifelong radical who must ponder whether a differently ordered society would have kept the murderesses under control, but is not at all sure that it would have been possible. He did not require this child-murder to maintain his conviction that "men are dangerous wild beasts." In the opinions expressed by the young Charles Eliot, we see this crime, and Auschwitz, becoming history. He sees his father as claiming false significance for the crime by relating it to Auschwitz, which "happened years before . . . [Charles] was born." He claims the right for himself and his generation to find out for themselves the "awful things" in the world of the here and now in which they stake their interest.

Without blaming the murder in *The Sleep of Reason* on any single factor, and despite the variety of reactions to the crime within Lewis Eliot's circle of friends, Snow nevertheless has clearly founded the novel on a defense of the life of reason against excessive cultivation of instinct. Its title is derived from a title of one of Goya's *Caprichos* etchings, "The sleep of reason brings forth monsters." In a late chapter, Lewis Eliot observes in a rare sermon directed to the reader:

> Reason was very weak as compared with instinct. Instinct was closer to the aboriginal sea out of which we had all climbed. Reason was a precarious structure. But, if we didn't use it to understand instinct, then there was no health in us at all.

Margaret said she had been brought up among people who believed it was easy to be civilized and rational. She had hated it. It made life too hygienic and too thin. But still, she had come to think even that was better than glorifying unreason.

The crime is clearly related to recent history in Eliot's peroration invoking the name of the novel: "Put reason to sleep, and all the stronger forces were let loose. We had seen that happen in our own lifetimes. In the world: and close to us."

Lewis Eliot's reference to Margaret's defense of civilized life despite her reservations about its quality recalls Miss Johnson's preference, in *On Iniquity*, for so-called bourgeois death over a life or death of violence. As the opinion of Eliot's wife, Margaret, harmonizes with his, so Miss Johnson is at one with her husband in urging that the suppression of instinct may have social value. Reversing William Blake's dictum, she observes, in criticizing a play depicting the murder of a child, that it is "better to nurse unacted desires than to strangle an infant in its cradle."

Strong support for these views is found in the words of a man often falsely accused of glorifying instinct, Sigmund Freud. Freud wrote, in his *Thoughts on War and Death:*

. . . if we are to be judged by the wishes in our unconscious, we are like a primitive man, simply a gang of murderers. It is well that all these wishes do not possess the potency which was attributed to them by primitive man; in the crossfire of mutual maledictions mankind would long since have perished, the best and wisest of men and the loveliest and fairest of women with the rest.

The sincerity of one's advocacy of the abolition of capital punishment would certainly be well tested by immersion in the details of the Moors Trial. In *On Iniquity* Pamela Hansford Johnson recalls in sharp detail the "exhilaration" of her attendance in the gallery of the House of Lords when capital punishment was finally abolished. She had the feeling "of a sudden cleansing and freshening: as if the windows had been thrown open upon a stuffy room, and the air of the sea had poured in." And yet she confesses that since life imprisonment was the maximum penalty Brady and Hindley faced, the trial provided no "catharsis," and "the end was, in fact, unaesthetic." She writes: " . . . something violent should have happened to put an end to violence. Throughout, we *were missing the shadow of the rope.*" Lewis Eliot has a similar impression during his attendance at the Ross-Pateman trial: "There was none of the pall upon the nerves, at the same time shameful and thrilling, which in those earlier murder trials I had sensed all round me and not been able to deny within myself. For there was no chance of these two being sent to their deaths."

No shame need be felt in recognizing the coexistence of an intellectual conviction that capital punishment is wrong and an irrational sense that the ritual of trial and punishment has suffered a psychological loss when violence remains unmet by counterviolence. Miss Johnson recognizes acutely that the observer may hope that the counterviolence will be provided not only by the ultimate penalty, but also by the trial itself. She admits to keen disappointment that nobody was able to break Hindley down in the course of the trial. Indeed, Miss Johnson is so dissatisfied with the purgative effects of the trial or the punishment of life imprisonment (with its attendant difficulty of security for the murderers, child-molesters being notoriously difficult to protect from their fellow prisoners) that she is compelled to conclude that it would have been better if Brady and Hindley had been caught red-handed and shot on the spot. In other words, the abolitionist ends by favoring instant capital punishment.

The confession of conflictive feelings by abolitionists of capital punishment is not new in our literature. We find a striking example in Thackeray. The complex links between Thackeray's attraction to public hanging and his abolitionist sentiments are the subject of my essay, "Why Thackeray Went to See a Man Hanged."

Thackeray finds in the emotions of the observer of executions a trace of *schadenfreude:* "There is something agreeable in the misfortunes of others, as the philosopher has told us." Although the reference may be to Lucretius or la Rochefoucauld, the observation is seconded by Finbow in Snow's *Death Under Sail:* "It is one of life's major consolations . . . the ease with which we bear other people's misfortunes."

An unusual alternative to capital punishment is proposed by Ian Capel, the protagonist of Snow's *Death Under Sail.* Shortly after the murder of their host on his boat, Capel proposes "another crime" to the assembled guests—that the murderer confess so that the guests can cooperatively arrange things to make the murder resemble suicide. Capel announces that he does not believe in "self-righteous revenge," which resembles the crime itself. His proposal, however, is made "on the single condition that whoever did it gets out of our company and our life, and does not come back."

In *The Sleep of Reason* many of Lewis Eliot's interlocutors and acquaintances are unhappy over the fact that the young murderesses, under the 1957 Homicide Act applicable to their trial, do not face capital punishment because they did not kill their victim by shooting. In the midst of the trial, Archibald Rose, the junior barrister for the prosecution, holds a party (a little hard to conceive, at least in this country) for all the lawyers in the case, including defense counsel and their juniors, and for others, of course including Lewis Eliot. When the conversation turns to capital punishment, a majority appears to favor its retention, including Mrs. Rose, who has just performed the maternal duties of putting the children to bed, but comes out in favor of capital punishment with "a firm young woman's confidence." Paradoxically, it is senior prosecuting counsel who comes out most strongly against capital punishment "even in a case like this."

Lewis Eliot himself is earlier faced with the capital punishment issue in a conversation with the C.I.D. officer who is in charge of the case. The officer does not believe in "the crap about deterrence," but supports capital punishment because "some people . . . aren't fit to live." Eliot replies: "We're not God, to say that." The officer then proceeds to voice an opinion that rings upon the ear strangely like that of Miss Johnson: ". . . when we had them in and discovered what they'd done, I'd have put a bullet in them both."

The end of this interview is unspectacular. When Eliot is asked what he would do with the murderers, he "had no answer ready, and gave no answer at all."

The refusal to give an answer on the issues of crime, its prevention or cure, is perhaps the respect in which Snow's work is most strongly set apart from his wife's essay. But both of them are equally convinced that intelligent people must live with and respond to the crimes and human disasters of their time. Perhaps one of the great civilizing benefits of the abolition of capital punishment will reside precisely in the destruction of the illusion that the violence of the crime has been wiped out by the violence of the execution and that the significance of the facts of the crime for the greater community has thereby been dispersed. No longer will the murderer, as proposed by Capel in *Death Under Sail*, "get out of our life"; we will be forced to continue to reflect on him and what he has done.

CHAPTER TWO

Dr. Jekyll and Mr. Stevenson

*Program notes for Cleveland Play House
production of* Dr. Jekyll and Mr. Hyde

In his essay "A Chapter on Dreams," Robert Louis Stevenson revealed that certain of the scenes of *The Strange Case of Dr. Jekyll and Mr. Hyde* (1886) and plot elements of much of his other fiction came to him in dreams. He amusingly referred to his "Brownies," the "little people" in his unconscious who had engaged in businesslike literary collaboration with him and were welcome successors to the "night-hag" who sent him frightening dreams when he was a child. Stevenson dreamed of Jekyll and Hyde in Bournemouth, England, while his body was racked with a fever following a lung hemorrhage and the delirium of his sleep's visions was possibly heightened by the drugs that his doctor had prescribed. Stevenson appears to have dreamed the idea of Jekyll and Hyde in great detail and clarity, and even attributed to his Brownies the invention of the powders that induced Dr. Jekyll's personality changes. He cried out in horror during his sleep, causing his wife, Fanny, to rouse him, "much to his indignation." He told her that he "was dreaming a fine bogey tale" and gave her a rapid sketch of Jekyll and Hyde up to the point when she had awakened him. At daybreak he passionately set to work on the story. He closeted himself in his sickroom for three days and then emerged with a completed thirty-thousand-word manuscript, which he read aloud to his wife and his stepson, Lloyd Osbourne. To his intense disappointment, Fanny was highly critical of his treatment of the story. She told him that he had trivialized the idea by writing a "thriller" and had failed to emphasize the allegorical message of his strange dream: that propensities for good and evil coexist uneasily in the human soul. "In the first draft," wrote Stevenson's official biographer, Graham Balfour, "Jekyll's nature was bad all through, and the Hyde change was worked only for the sake of a disguise." Fanny's appraisal of her husband's work was not always reliable, but in this instance Stevenson recognized the justice of her comments; he threw the manuscript into the fire. His action was not one of artistic pique, for he immediately proceeded to rewrite the story in the vein Fanny had suggested and did not want his creativity to be inhibited by excessive use of the original draft. After three more days of work, according to Fanny's account, the second manuscript of *Dr. Jekyll* was completed and, after six weeks of polishing, it was given to Stevenson's publishers and to the world. The book's success was immediate. It pleased Queen Victoria, became the theme of church sermons, sold forty thousand copies during the first six months, and was adapted by a number of playwrights.

The unusually clear dream vision of Jekyll and Hyde and the terror it inspired in the thirty-six-year-old Stevenson suggest that the idea had a strong root in Stevenson's personality. From biographical data and the comments of Stevenson's contemporaries, we are able to determine that this was indeed the case and that the concept of an outwardly respectable man leading a double life whose dark side included immorality or even crime preoccupied Stevenson from his early childhood.

The image of Jekyll and Hyde appears to have had its origin in a real personage of Stevenson's native city of Edinburgh—Deacon Brodie (1741–1788). William Brodie was a successful carpenter and cabinetmaker and so highly regarded in his craft that he became "deacon" or president of the Edinburgh carpenters' trade. Far from having the solid churchgoing habits that his title might suggest to those unacquainted with its professional significance, Deacon Brodie spent many happy hours on Sunday mornings making wax impressions of the door locks of friends and neighbors who were at services. For Brodie led a double life—by day he pursued his carpentry, and at night he was a daring housebreaker. The houses and offices he raided (at first alone and later as leader of a gang of three other men) included many he had previously visited to make repairs or perform other work of his trade. Between blows of hammer and strokes of saw he had taken the opportunity to make copies of keys and locks and to observe room arrangements and the arrival and departure schedules of inhabitants and workers. Some victims who witnessed his nighttime incursions thought they recognized him under his black gauze mask, but kept their own counsel, out of either friendship or disbelief. The next morning Brodie would condole with them on their losses or would be in attendance at the town council, of which he was an ex officio member, helping formulate plans to catch the audacious criminal. Brodie's career ended when a member of his gang gave him away to the authorities after a disappointing raid on the Scottish Excise Office. Brodie fled and was caught in Holland, where he was making profitable use of his fugitive hours learning the art of forgery from an itinerant expert.

The Deacon was hanged in 1788 at the Edinburgh Tolbooth Prison. Legend has it that he was hanged on a gallows that he had built in the course of his carpentry for the city, but unfortunately this supreme irony is not borne out by chronology.

Deacon Brodie seized on the imagination of his townspeople and they have never forgotten him. In addition to the fascination of his double life, it was obvious to the people of Edinburgh that he was not attracted to crime primarily by love of gain, although it cannot have been inexpensive to support his passion for cockfighting and gambling and to maintain the three separate households he shared with his wife and two mistresses (and a total of at least five children). Surely it was a streak of romanticism that inspired his theft of the official mace from the College Library. He was a dandy, and saw himself in a dramatic light. He sang airs from John Gay's *Beggar's Opera* on the night of the Excise Office raid and in his last days in prison, leading a local newspaper to comment that he apparently identified himself with Captain Macheath and to advocate the banning of Gay's play from the stage.

In the night nursery where Robert Louis Stevenson slept as a child were a bookcase and a chest of drawers made by Deacon Brodie. There is little doubt that his devoted nurse, Alison Cunningham ("Cummie"), who had the odd notion that the way to put an impressionable child to sleep is to tell him terrifying stories, regaled him with the exploits of Edinburgh's famous Deacon. When Stevenson was thirteen or fourteen years old, he made his first attempt at a play based on Deacon Brodie, and at nineteen, in 1869, he wrote a later draft. In 1879 his friend W. E. Henley, the hot-tempered, red-bearded, one-legged poet and critic who was to serve as the model for one of Stevenson's immortal characters, Long John Silver, "fished" the 1869 draft out of a trunk and persuaded Stevenson to collaborate with him on a new version. In their play, Deacon Brodie pursues his burglar's trade partly for the economic purpose of restoring his sister's dowry, which he had dissipated by gambling. At the same time, Stevenson and Henley introduce a philosophical interpretation which is underscored by the play's subtitle, "The Double Life." Deacon Brodie feels that his "naked self" is stifled by the social restrictions and hypocrisy of daytime Edinburgh, and leaps into his nights of crime as into a "new life." He invokes the night as "the grimy, cynical night that makes all cats grey, and all honesties of one complexion."

When at the end of the play the Deacon, in a departure from his historical fate, dies in a duel with the police, he cries that he has found the "new life" at last. Unfortunately, *Deacon Brodie*, like Stevenson's other dramatic collaborations with Henley, was unsuccessful, and its American performances were not helped by the fact that Henley's brother, an untalented actor, was cast in the title role.

The disappointing fate of the play by no means ended Stevenson's fascination with the figure of Deacon Brodie or his speculations about the existence of the unknown dark sides of men whose public characters were beyond reproach. Eve Blantyre Simpson, the sister of Stevenson's close friend Walter Simpson, reports that Stevenson would pace up and down before the Simpsons' library fire, and would "expatiate on the double life, speaking again of the Deacon. He would wonder what burglary some esteemed citizen of his own day was guilty of in the . . . [night]."

The respected Dr. Henry Jekyll and his alter ego, the unspeakable Mr. Hyde, are the permanent embodiment of Stevenson's obsession with the double soul of man. To a modern generation, which has learned only relatively recently, through such studies as Steven Marcus's *The Other Victorians*, of the unpleasant aspects of the private conduct of the Victorians, Stevenson's tale seems to be as well suited to nineteenth-century England as to Deacon Brodie's Edinburgh of a century earlier. In fact, in a striking exception to the rule that history never repeats itself, a notorious criminal case was tried at Sheffield in 1879 that presented a close parallel to the exploits of Brodie. Charlie Peace—known to his suburban community in London as "Mr. Thompson," a proper, violin-playing citizen, busy with his great assortment of pets, a regular attendant at parish church services and an outspoken critic of the pro-Turkish policies of the government—was a professional housebreaker by night. When he was arrested in the course of a burglary, his identity was discovered and it was found that he had committed two murders, one of them years before. Peace was hanged for his crimes and his violin is now one of the prime exhibits in Scotland Yard's Black Museum.

Yet it is possible that Jekyll and Hyde had a far more personal meaning for Stevenson than as a commentary on Victorian hypocrisy or a re-creation of Edinburgh's criminal history. After the overlay of make-up and illusion of the film and stage presentations of Jekyll and Hyde is removed, and one returns to Stevenson's original, it is striking to note that Mr. Hyde was not physically monstrous. He looked human, but those who saw him found something indefinably repellent in his appearance; something in his countenance and manner set him apart at the first glance. As Mr. Enfield observed, "There is something wrong with his appearance, something displeasing, something downright detestable. I never saw a man I so disliked, and yet I scarce know why." Significantly, Hyde is also described in the story as "much smaller, slighter and younger than Henry Jekyll," and Hyde dresses "in a fashion that would have made an ordinary person laughable; his clothes, although they were of rich and sober fabric, were enormously too large for him in every measurement—the trousers hanging on his legs and rolled up to keep them from the ground, the waist of the coat below his haunches, and the collar sprawling wide upon his shoulders." In Jekyll's statement of the case, which concludes the story, the doctor confesses that looking upon the ugly Hyde in the mirror, he "was conscious of no repugnance. This, too, was myself." Jekyll explains Hyde's youth and puniness as due to the fact that the evil side of his character represented by Hyde was less robust and developed because of the restrictions of virtue and control to which Hyde had been subjected until he was finally given supremacy. However, when we recall that the vision of Jekyll and Hyde came to Stevenson full-born out of his dreams, there is room for speculation that the small size and youth of Hyde had even greater meaning. Stevenson as a young student in Edinburgh had led a rakish life in the unsavory quarters of his city, and his Bohemian conduct caused him difficulty with his parents. From the black velvet jacket (given to him by his father) that he wore during his adventures, he was given the nickname "Velvet Coat" by the sailors, sweeps, thieves and prostitutes with whom he consorted. He must have looked back at that period with considerable shame and it may not be too much to suggest that the dwarfish Mr. Hyde in his rich clothes has a close kinship with Stevenson's deepest memories of his own young manhood.

Although Stevenson was amused by the speed with which the phrase "Jekyll and Hyde" passed into the language as a shorthand expression for split personality, there may be some poignancy as well as humor in his having signed a letter to his beloved mother shortly after the appearance of his famous tale: "I hope, Jekyll, I fear, Hyde."

CHAPTER THREE

Why Thackeray Went
to See a Man Hanged

Critics of Thackeray generally assign him a negative role in the history of crime literature. Major emphasis is placed on his persistent and resourceful opposition to the crime fiction of the 1830s and 1840s, the so-called Newgate novels. The Newgate controversy is certainly an attractive phenomenon, since it not only brought into conflict some of the leading literary figures of the early Victorian period, but also illumined fundamental disagreements as to the scope of subject matter appropriate for fiction and the responsibility of the author to define his relationship to his immoral characters. However, the customary portrayal of Thackeray as savage critic of crime fiction should not be permitted to obscure his own interest in crime or his affirmative contributions to the literature of crime, particularly his writings against capital punishment, "The Case of Peytel" (1839) and "Going to See a Man Hanged" (1840).

The "Newgate" tag was intended to disparage a number of novels, published in England between 1830 and 1847, which in the view of their critics presented crime and criminals in an appealing or sentimentalized manner. In Professor Keith Hollingsworth's words, "a Newgate novel was one in which an important character came (or, if imaginary, might have come) out of the Newgate Calendar." The Newgate

Calendar, which had appeared in various versions since the early eighteenth century, was a collection of biographies of English criminals, including many famous in legend and literature, such as the highwayman Dick Turpin, the burglar and jailbreaker Jack Sheppard, the fence and informer Jonathan Wild. However, the common denominator of a Newgate or pseudo-Newgate character brought together under the guns of Thackeray and other critics very disparate works. The Newgate novels of Harrison Ainsworth, *Rookwood* (1834), featuring Turpin as its hero, and *Jack Sheppard* (1839), romanticized highwayman and thief in narratives highly charged with Gothic elements and spiced by the author's concoction of underworld or "flash" dialect. The principal target of the anti-Newgate critics was a series of novels by Edward Bulwer-Lytton, including *Eugene Aram* (1832), a sympathetic portrait of a brilliant scholar who murders out of utilitarian impulses. The book was loosely based on the career of a schoolteacher who was executed in 1759 for a murder committed many years before. Unlike Ainsworth's mindless romances, many of Bulwer's crime novels, notably *Paul Clifford* (1830), were intended as critiques of social injustice and a legal system that was structured and administered in favor of the privileged class. However, Bulwer's books were marred by an overblown style and pretensions to intellectual and philosophical realms beyond the author's powers of flight.

Charles Dickens's *Oliver Twist* (1838–1839) was also treated by Thackeray as a Newgate novel, although it appears to keep strange company with the works of Ainsworth and Bulwer-Lytton. The reading public, apparently in accord with Dickens's intention, identified Fagin with a notorious pickpocket, Isaac or Ikey Solomon, but Dickens, not only in the heat of the critical controversy that ensued, but in the pages of the novel itself, took pains to disassociate *Oliver* from Newgate fiction. Unlike Ainsworth or Bulwer, Dickens did not evoke sympathy for his criminals. Bill Sikes is a horror, and if Fagin is occasionally appealing in his relations with Oliver and the other boys in his gang, he is only so in contrast to the more brutal keepers of the workhouse in which Oliver spent his first years. Moreover, in two passages, one serious and one satiric, Dickens separates the real lives of his characters from the bloody histories of the Newgate Calendars. It will be recalled that Fagin frightened Oliver at bedtime by having him read "a history of the lives and trials of great criminals" and that Oliver thrust the book from him and "prayed Heaven to spare him from such deeds." In a humorous vein, Dickens later has Charley Bates express concern that the Artful Dodger's trial record will not accurately reflect the Dodger's professional competence. "How will he stand in the Newgate Calendar?" laments Charley. "P'raps not be there at all."

Thackeray's role in the Newgate controversy was decisive. By a series of literary assaults, he put an end to the spate of Newgate novels. Ainsworth and Bulwer-Lytton turned to other subjects. Although Dickens continued to use criminal subject matter throughout his works, including his last, unfinished novel, *The Mystery of Edwin Drood,* he was too strong a writer to succumb to Thackeray's campaign, and in any event, many of Thackeray's criticisms did not find a mark in Dickens's treatment of crime. Thackeray's anti-Newgate writings included a number of critical barbs and satires directed against Bulwer, culminating in his parody of *Eugene Aram,* entitled "George de Barnwell," published in *Punch* in 1847. Thackeray's major attack on Newgate fiction was made through his comic novel *Catherine,* which appeared in installments in *Fraser's Magazine,* 1839–1840. In this novel, Thackeray, instead of parodying a work of a Newgate adversary, dipped into the pages of the Newgate Calendar to find a criminal who would be much more revolting than any whom Ainsworth or Bulwer had glorified. He hit on Catherine Hayes, wife of a London tradesman, who conspired with two lodgers, including one who may have been her illegitimate son, to murder her husband. This lurid biography, which features beheading and dismemberment of the victim, and burning of Catherine alive at the stake, is described in the 1828 edition of the Newgate Calendar as "altogether too shocking for a single comment." Thackeray's budding skill as a novelist overcame his original satiric intent and the plot of *Catherine* is elaborated far beyond the facts of the case. But Thackeray interspersed passages satirizing Bulwer's purple passages and Ainsworth's Gothic scenes, and to include Dickens within his sights, he published the work under the pseudonym Ikey Solomons, Esq., Jr., a slight modification of the name of Fagin's "original." As he was later to do in his mature novels, Thackeray intruded into the pages of the novel *in propria persona*. In his interpolated commentaries he attacked the Newgate novels by name. He ridiculed the "white-washed saint" of *Oliver Twist* under the nasalized epithet "poor Biss Dadsy" and criticized Dickens for using his writing power to create interest in "a set of ruffians whose occupations are thievery, murder, and prostitution."

Enemies of Thackeray among the critical ranks (and their name is legion) often explain his anti-Newgate campaign by his personal dislike of Bulwer and his willingness to take up the cudgels of *Fraser's Magazine* in its quarrel with Bulwer, which had originated in the early 1830s. Such an assessment does Thackeray an injustice. The views that Thackeray expressed in the Newgate controversy are fully consistent with his strong personal beliefs as to the proper relationship between crime and literature, beliefs he voiced throughout his career and in contexts that did not involve the literary personalities whom he attacked as Newgate novelists.

In approaching a definition of Thackeray's attitude toward crime literature, one must begin with the patent fact that Thackeray was very interested in crime. In this he was not to be distinguished from most of the literary figures of his period, including the Newgate novelists. In 1832, in the early days of his journalistic career, Thackeray wrote that to news-papermen "a good murder is a godsend," and proceeded to list their favorites among nineteenth-century murderers— Corder, Cook, Burke, Bishop and Williams, and especially Thurtell. In rating murderers in terms of quality, Thackeray's newspapermen were following in the footsteps of Thomas De Quincey, who had given ironic sanction to the application of aesthetic standards to the study of crime in his essays "On Murder Considered as One of the Fine Arts," of which the first appeared in 1827. Thackeray, like De Quincey, was well-versed in the criminal annals of England, from which his heroine Catherine Hayes had been drawn. More-over, Thackeray had equal familiarity with the analogous collections of French criminal cases which were published in various series bearing the name *Causes Célèbres.* Thackeray not only deemed criminal cases worthy of private study and enjoyment, but like De Quincey and Defoe before him, he put his hand to the recounting of a criminal career. Among the pieces published in his *Paris Sketch Book* of 1840 appears Thackeray's witty and beautifully written account of epi-sodes from the life of Cartouche, a famous eighteenth-cen-tury French thief, murderer and confidence man. At the beginning of the essay, Thackeray deftly associates his under-taking with the popularity of the Newgate fiction in England. He observes that "as Newgate and the highways are so much the fashion with us in England, we may be allowed to look abroad for histories of a similar tendency." With a sure hand, Thackeray proceeds to sketch a succession of comic scenes from Cartouche's quicksilver career, climaxing with his wed-ding, in the guise of a fictitious count, with a supposedly wealthy widow, whose noble retinue is discovered to include a fence and a bordello-keeper. Unlike the passionate New-gate novelists, Thackeray, through humor, keeps himself at a distance from the crimes he is describing. In this detach-ment he follows the manner of De Quincey, and in his ironic ranking of Cartouche among the "great" men of history, imitates Fielding's *Jonathan Wild*, which he admired.

It is also obvious that Thackeray considered criminal themes, if properly handled, an appropriate subject for novels as well as nonfiction. Almost all Thackeray's early fiction is concerned with rogues making their selfish way through society over the heads of dupes and in the shelter of social pretense and snobbery. The supreme rogue is Becky Sharp herself. It is not always remembered by the readers of *Vanity Fair* that Becky Sharp caps her career of knavery by the murder of Jos Sedley. The way for this ultimate crime is prepared by Thackeray in Chapter LI, describing Becky's triumph in a charade as Clytemnestra murdering Agamemnon. In a scene pictured by Thackeray in an illustration entitled "The Triumph of Clytemnestra," Becky takes her bow with a large dagger still clasped in her hand. The Clytemnestra theme is taken up again in Thackeray's illustration for the last chapter of the book, where Becky is shown lurking behind a curtain with a cruel expression on her face, eavesdropping on Dobbin's conversation with Jos Sedley. Thackeray captioned the illustration "Becky's Second Appearance in the Character of Clytemnestra." The murder accusation against Becky Sharp is made much more explicit. Dobbin had gone to see Jos Sedley, and encouraged him to leave Becky Sharp, since he had been alarmed by reports that Becky had heavily insured Sedley's life. Jos was afraid to leave Becky and shortly thereafter died under mysterious circumstances, which led the insurance company representatives to declare that they had never seen such a black case. Their attempts to resist payment to Becky are overawed by her experienced legal advisers, the firm of Burke, Thurtell and Hayes, which bears the names of three famous nineteenth-century murderers, including Thackeray's old favorite, Catherine Hayes.

Thackeray's position in the Newgate controversy therefore cannot be explained by his distaste for the subject of crime or for its portrayal in literature. His attack on the

Newgate writers stemmed from his disapproval of their glo-
rification and sentimentalization of criminals, criminal acts
and low life. He believed that fiction and the art of writing
had an educational function. In a letter to his mother in 1839
regarding the popularity of dramatic adaptations of *Jack
Sheppard,* he appeared to express the belief that the romantic portrayal of crime is capable of inducing imitative criminal conduct. He wrote that at one of the theaters where *Jack
Sheppard* was playing, vendors were hawking throughout
the lobbies so-called Sheppard bags, including picklocks and
an assortment of burglary equipment. He added that two
young gentlemen had confessed that they had been induced
to take up burglary because of the attractions of the play.
However, his objections to the glamorization of crime went
beyond the possibility that printed or acted words can have
antisocial effects on conduct. The presentation of crime and
the underworld in a falsely attractive light was simply bad
moral teaching. In his view, the good novelist must distinguish virtuous characters from the vicious and must make his
own judgments on them plain. This stricture applied to
fictional treatment not only of crime, but of sexual conduct
as well, and in the latter realm Thackeray even came to find
that the obvious affection of Henry Fielding for Tom Jones
was a fault to be forgiven in so great a master, but not to be
imitated. Another basis for Thackeray's criticism of the Newgate writers was that they did not know the milieu of which
they wrote from their own experience, and therefore were
not equipped to add the necessary corrective elements of
misery and squalor. Thackeray was prepared to admit that
there were quite likely virtues in the real-life equivalents of
Dickens's Nancy, but held that since Dickens could not possibly know firsthand Nancy's shortcomings and vices, he was
wrong to present his public with a partial portrait.

Thackeray's horror of glamorized crime, far from being
invented to lash English competitors, was also evidenced by
his responses to French fiction and drama. In 1843 he de-

scribed Eugène Sue's *The Mysteries of Paris* as "thieves' literature" and gave thanks for the cessation of similar literature
in England. Two years later he referred to Sue's novel as one
of the most immoral books in the world. In his review of
French drama in *The Paris Sketch Book* he also expressed his
disgust with the murders, adulteries and other offenses
which were put forward appealingly as the standard fare of
the dramas of Hugo and Dumas.

It is a paradox of literary history that at the very time
Thackeray was leveling his attacks against the crime novelists, he was making his own most important contribution to
crime literature and history, namely, his essays of 1839 and
1840 in favor of the abolition of capital punishment. This
aspect of Thackeray's career has been relatively ignored, in
comparison both with his role in the Newgate controversy
and with Dickens's role several years later among the advocates of abolition. However, no other facet of Thackeray's
career is more deeply rooted in his background and personality. Throughout his life, Thackeray appears to have been
obsessed with capital punishment, both as a horrifying physical fact capable of arousing morbid fascination and, at the
same time, as a personal issue intimately related to his own
speculations about the meaning of life and death, health and
illness, and divine involvement in human affairs.

Thackeray spent several years of his London youth amid
the names and symbols of butchery and hanging. When he
was between the ages of eleven and seventeen, he attended
the Charterhouse School, which was located close to the
Smithfield Market, the principal slaughtering yards of London, and to Newgate Prison, where men were hanged, to the
delectation of the public. For many years after leaving the
school, and well into middle age, Thackeray was accustomed
to refer to his alma mater as the "Slaughterhouse," a pun that
may have been derived from the school's propinquity to
Smithfield, but would also have been justified by the cruel
regime imposed on Charterhouse students by whipping; the

institutionalized but unregulated aggression of fellow students; and the calculated brutality of the headmaster. Fiction of Thackeray's reflects the central role of flogging in his school life, and he gives one of his fictional schoolteachers the ominous name Dr. Birch. It is not unfair to speculate as to whether the brutality of English public school life could not have combined with the institution of public hanging to contribute to the preoccupation of Thackeray and many of his contemporaries with criminal punishment.

There is no reason to believe that Thackeray attended a public hanging during his stay at the Charterhouse School. The first references to public hangings in his correspondence are made in letters to his mother from Cambridge in 1829. In recounting the events of the week of March 22, he wrote that the assize judges had taken up their traditional residence at Trinity College and that "the court was thronged with little boys & girls to behold the mighty men as they passed to the Judgement." In an entry in the same letter made several days later, he noted that the judges had departed and that the criminals were awaiting sentence. He did not know whether any of them would be hanged, but in any event, he had not, like some men he knew, arranged for a breakfast party to see them hanged. This first acquaintance with the aficionados of hanging was still in his mind a decade later. In his novel *Catherine* the Hayes family are pictured as enthusiastic attenders of public hangings. Thackeray comments in an aside:

I can recollect, when I was a gyp at Cambridge, that the "men" used to have breakfast-parties for the same purpose; and the exhibition of the morning acted infallibly upon the stomach, and caused the young students to eat with much voracity.

Thackeray's reaction to hanging in his college days establishes the pattern that was to mark his career, an obvious fascination with the subject accompanied by a reluctance to become a spectator.

Thackeray's interest in executions bloomed in the foster-
ing air of France. In 1836, during his residence in Paris,
where he had been studying art and was beginning to try his
hand at journalism, Thackeray made unsuccessful efforts to
attend two executions. The first was that of Giuseppe Fieschi,
who had participated in an unsuccessful assassination conspiracy against Louis Philippe. The assassins attacked a royal
procession with a rapid-firing "infernal machine" of Fieschi's
manufacture. Though the king merely suffered a grazed el-
bow, about twenty people, including spectators, were killed.
The day for Fieschi's death was purposely kept secret and he
was executed in some remote quarter of Paris. Thackeray
therefore missed the execution, but was revolted by the car-
nival-time crowd that scoured the city hoping to crown its
merrymaking with the sight of Fieschi's guillotining. Several
weeks later, Thackeray set out to witness the execution of
Lacenaire, the nihilist murderer, whom many will recall as
the sinister villain of the film *Children of Paradise*. This time,
arriving too late for the execution, Thackeray came upon a
group of street boys dancing in triumph around a little pool
of ice tinged with the blood of Lacenaire and his accomplice
Avril, who had been guillotined with him.

These experiences did not immediately inspire Thackeray
to record them, but they remained vivid in his memory and
imagination. In 1839 they came rushing forth under the impulse of a new French case of crime and punishment, the
case of Sebastian Peytel.

Peytel, a *notaire* of the town of Belley, was tried and executed for the murder of his wife and their servant, Louis
Rey. The case has a certain amount of the inevitable interest
that is engendered by a family murder involving middle-
class people well known to a closely knit community. However, much of the Parisian furor over the Peytel case was
artificially aroused by the intervention of Honoré de Balzac
in behalf of Peytel, whom he had met while Peytel was serving as theater critic on a journal with a prophetically criminal

name, *Le Voleur.* Balzac, competitive soul that he was, was eager to attach his name to the defense of a *cause célèbre,* as Voltaire had done in the Calas case. To Thackeray's credit, it cannot be said that his interest in Peytel was aroused by either literary fashion or journalistic loyalty. Thackeray equivocated as to his personal belief in Peytel's innocence, but felt strongly that the evidence on which he was convicted was insufficient and unduly magnified by the force of community prejudice. He did not argue, as Balzac had done in substance, that Peytel must be innocent because he was a literary man of a sort. Thackeray had a low opinion of the letter Balzac had published in defense of Peytel. This letter, Thackeray wrote, was "so very long, so very dull, so very pompous, promising so much, and performing so little, that the Parisian public gave up Peytel and his case altogether."

Peytel's wife had been shot on the Lyons Road during a nocturnal trip in a coach driven by her husband, and their servant, who had accompanied them in a separate vehicle, was found lying dead nearby, the victim of a proverbial "blunt instrument." It was Peytel's story that the servant, Rey, had fired at his wife from a distance in an attempt to rob the Peytels of a sum of money they were carrying with them and that Peytel had pursued the servant and struck murderous blows in retribution. Public opinion said otherwise and held Peytel guilty of the deliberate murder of an unwelcome spouse on whom he had already perpetrated financial frauds, as well as of the servant, who was reputed to have formed the third component of the family triangle so dear to French theatergoers. To Thackeray, the prosecution in the case smacked too much of the theater. The act of prosecution, from which he quoted at length in his article, was written in the spirit of a melodrama, in which Peytel emerged as the villain and the victims were romanticized. Thackeray was particularly shocked by the prosecution's references to the disbelief of Peytel's defense by the community. We know Thackeray's low opinion of crime in the French theater and he thought no better of the introduction of theater into French crime. His article contains his own mock dramatis personae, in which he lists the principal personages in the case, with a description of the stock characters the prosecution sought to assign them.

A major portion of Thackeray's article was devoted to a point-by-point demonstration that the factual inferences on which the prosecution and conviction were based could be reversed and made to favor Peytel. Although Thackeray's argument does not appear to be completely convincing—particularly in his overlooking the powder burns on the face of Madame Peytel, which countered Peytel's story that Rey had fired from a distance—his performance is impressive enough to induce some regret that he never tried his hand at detective fiction. Indeed, his most ingenious suggestion—that Rey might have shot at Madame Peytel mistaking her for her husband, since she was wrapped in his cloak—anticipates quite competently the "wrong victim" formula of the modern detective story.

Peytel was executed in October 1839, in Bourg. Thackeray did not attend the execution, but quoted a report of Peytel's last days and his execution from a French newspaper. The principal focus of Thackeray's commentary on Peytel's death is on capital punishment as the cruel result of an inflammatory prosecution that may have sent an innocent man to his death. After the quotation of the newspaper account, Thackeray broadens his attack on capital punishment. He raises the question whether any "single person, meditating murder, would be deterred therefrom by beholding this—nay, a thousand more executions." He theorizes that capital punishment is psychologically rooted in man's blood lust and is related to other forms of entertainment providing a release for the delight in blood. He recalls the excitement the audience feels at a new tragedy on the stage and the joy at the first drawing of blood at a wrestling or boxing match.

As his vision of the function of capital punishment widens,

Thackeray remembers the carnival rabble that hunted for Fieschi's guillotine and the urchins who danced around the blood of Lacenaire. In the light of these memories, he realizes that execution proceeds not only from blood lust, but from a pleasure in the misfortunes of fellow men, a human trait that had been observed by Lucretius and la Rochefoucauld. This malicious joy leads men, Thackeray writes, to enjoy a good breakfast after an execution, to "cut jokes" upon it. He is led on to make a peroration in which the principal arguments against capital punishment are swiftly and powerfully made:

> But, for God's sake, if we are to enjoy this, let us do so in moderation; and let us, at least, be sure of a man's guilt before we murder him. To kill him, even with the full assurance that he is guilty, is hazardous enough . . . What use is there in killing him? You deter no one else from committing the crime by so doing; you give us, to be sure, half an hour's pleasant entertainment; but it is a great question whether we derive much moral profit from the sight. If you want to keep a murderer from further inroads upon society, are there not plenty of hulks and prisons . . . ? Above all, . . . can any man declare positively and upon oath, that Peytel was guilty, and that this was not *the third murder* in the family?

It appears that Thackeray's perceptions of the injustice of executions were internalized to a remarkable extent and became inextricably involved with his own personal traits and religious outlook. His preoccupation with execution as a dramatic event of suffering was probably related to his strong anxieties about death and illness. From an early age he was the victim of apparently psychosomatic symptoms, which were followed by a series of physical ills that were only too real. While at Charterhouse School he began to suffer from severe headaches, which have been attributed by Dr. Chester M. Jones of Harvard University to a nervous origin associated with unjust treatment by the headmaster. He continued to suffer painful headaches during his lifetime, as well as a painful stricture of the urethra and digestive problems aggravated by intemperance. His concern with his own ills seemed to translate itself to an acute empathy for the physical suffering of others. This tendency can only have been sharpened by the death of his infant daughter Jane in March 1839. In addition to his physical sensitivity, he was constantly moved to rebellion against his mother's fundamentalist conviction that all ills were visited by a retributive God.

The link of these personal preoccupations with Thackeray's developing views on capital punishment can be seen in his revealing letter to his mother written in late December 1839, one month after his article on Peytel. Thackeray begins in a melancholy mood induced by news he has received that a friend, Salt, is near death from consumption. As is his wont, he immediately thinks of his own happier state and of the religious implications of "unequal lots." He announces his belief that God represents an Abstract Good that does not determine, but transcends, defects in material things such as illness, pain, sorrow and crime. The conclusion follows that God does not repay material sin by vengeance on the immortal soul. With an ironic sideswipe at his generation's overweening faith in science, which satisfied him no more than fundamentalism, he remarked: "Judas Iscariot came into the world with diseases from his mother, and phrenological bumps—who shall visit the sins of his carcass upon his immortal soul?" (The humor of this remark is enhanced when it is recalled that the phrenologist who examined Lacenaire had found "bumps of benevolence and religious veneration.") Applying to human affairs his doctrine that divine justice does not punish or deter crime, Thackeray expresses his view that there is no moral basis for criminal sanctions. "One act of violence is not right because it has been preceded by another," he wrote; "philosophically and religiously we have no right to retaliate but we are obliged to make such bargains and compromises for peace & quietness' sake."

In 1840 Thackeray's tortuous path of several years was at last to lead him to a public hanging, the execution of the valet

Courvoisier for the murder of his master, Lord William Russell. In May Thackeray wrote to his mother that the murder (which had occurred on May 6) was a nuisance and that "the stupid town talks about nothing else." Despite Thackeray's professed distaste for the case, he was persuaded to attend the execution of Courvoisier in the company of Richard Monckton Milnes, poet and member of Parliament, who had recently voted in favor of an unsuccessful motion by William Ewart to abolish capital punishment. He put on a brave front the day before the hanging, writing to Milnes declining an invitation to stay up with him all night and instead most strongly recommending "sleep as a preparative to the day's pleasures."

Shortly after the execution, Thackeray wrote to his mother in a very depressed mood. He began his letter with a response to his mother's report of the illness of a friend, and added the insightful comment that "I am . . . always beginning speaking of myself, when another's misfortunes or danger are spoken of." He then shifts to the subject of the Courvoisier hanging, which clearly has contributed to his low spirits:

I have been to see Courvoisier hanged & am miserable ever since. I can't do my work and yet work must be done for the poor babbies' sake. It is most curious the effect his death has had on me, and I am trying to work it off in a paper on the subject. Meanwhile it weighs upon the mind, like cold plum pudding on the stomach, & as soon as I begin to write, I get melancholy.

The paper to which Thackeray referred in his letter was starkly titled "Going to See a Man Hanged" and was originally published in *Fraser's Magazine*. Thackeray begins his account with an imaginative reconstruction of the night before the hanging, which strongly contrasts the "unequal lots" of the participants in the drama and of those Londoners who pass the night unaware of the coming execution: the sleepless Thackeray; Monckton Milnes, who stayed up all night at his club in the hilarious company of an eminent wit; the anonymous dying rich and poor surrounded by weeping friends and "solemn oily doctors"; and the resigned Courvoisier, who has no duties left to fulfill but a letter to his mother and disposition of his miserable property.

Monckton Milnes calls for Thackeray in his carriage and the trip to Snow Hill and Newgate Prison is described. Thackeray does not entrust to words the first visual impact the gallows made on him, but instead drew a solid black rectangle surmounted by a thick-lined frame and the noose rings. As the sight of the gallows defeated Thackeray's pen, so the balance of the narrative of the execution appears to consist largely of a series of subjective diversions from the facts of the experience. Thackeray comments on the insignificance of political decisions as compared with the immovable mass of the crowd. He remarks favorably on the good behavior of the common people and their festive mood, which appear to please him more than the riotousness of the French. He even spots two girls who put him in mind of Dickens's Miss Nancy. But when the moment of the hanging arrives, a moment with which he had been flirting since 1836, he learns as much about himself as about the event he came to see:

I am not ashamed to say that I could look no more, but shut my eyes as the last dreadful act was going on, which sent this wretched, guilty soul into the presence of God.

As in the Peytel article, the greatness of Thackeray's "Going to See a Man Hanged" lies in its eloquent peroration. The second article marks an advance in Thackeray's emotional response because he is satisfied that Courvoisier was guilty of murder. Yet the experience left Thackeray with "an extraordinary feeling of terror and shame," springing from his partaking with forty thousand others in "this hideous debauchery, which is more exciting than sleep, or than wine, or the last new ballet."

In accord with his lifelong religious disputations with his

mother, Thackeray hotly denies that it is natural that when a man has killed he should be killed. He notes that man has rejected the lesser compensations of Mosaic law, an eye for an eye, a tooth for a tooth, but retained the most terrible, a life for a life. He reserves his final barb for the deterrence theory. His point drives home in a magnificently spare sentence which echoes the conclusion of the Peytel article, but universalizes his condemnation of capital punishment by rendering irrelevant the guilt of the hanged man:

I fully confess that I came away down Snow Hill that morning with a disgust for murder, but it was for *the murder I saw done*.

The same equation of the crimes of murderer and executioner is made in *The Irish Sketch Book* (1843). Commenting on the report in a Dublin newspaper of the death sentences of two convicted murderers, Thackeray writes:

I confess, for my part, to that common cant and sickly sentimentality, which, thank God! is felt by a great number of people nowadays, and which leads them to revolt against murder, whether performed by a ruffian's knife or a hangman's rope: whether accompanied with a curse from the thief as he blows his victim's brains out, or a prayer from my lord on the bench in his wig and black cap.

Thackeray's outcries against capital punishment were spontaneous reactions to his experiences in the late 1830s and early 1840s, and did not recur. However, his tactful wrangles with his mother over her evangelical attachment to the doctrine of divine retribution continued unabated throughout his lifetime, and he displayed special energy in expressing his views to his daughters when his mother attempted to indoctrinate them. His fiction abounds in scenes of execution, including the famous "Princess's Tragedy" chapter of *Barry Lyndon,* which was omitted from Stanley Kubrick's film version. In Thackeray's correspondence there are scattered mentions of hanging, generally in a light vein. It is not clear whether we should attribute callousness or embarrassment to Thackeray's letter (in French) to Mrs. Ir-

vine in 1848, in which he apologetically reports that he is to
dine at Newgate the next day with the Sheriffs of London and
that they are to see the prisoners, the treadmills and the
"jolis petits condamnés" who are to be hanged. Only a small
portion of capital criminals were actually executed in Victorian England, but the inappropriate frivolousness of Thackeray's reference still strikes a discordant note. Later in 1848
Thackeray mentions in a letter to Reverend Brookfield his
visit to a favorite haunt, the Cyder Cellars, "to hear the man
sing about going to be hanged." The song to which Thackeray referred was the ballad of the condemned chimney
sweep Sam Hall, which was then the rage in London. There
is an intriguing possibility that even in these apparently triv-
ial letters, as in his cheerful note to Milnes on the eve of
Courvoisier's hanging, Thackeray's more troubled responses
to hangings may have been close to the surface. He notes that
after his entertainment by the ballad singer he returned
home with a headache.

It is justly observed of Thackeray that he was not a reformer. His sympathies were more easily engaged by individuals than by ideas or causes. During his visit to America
in 1853 it was his first impression that the miseries of slavery
had been greatly exaggerated by the abolitionists. But when
he met Harriet Beecher Stowe he found to his surprise that
she was "a gentle, almost pretty, person, with a very great
sweetness in her eyes." He added, in a letter to Mrs. Baxter:

I am sure she must be good and truth-telling from her face and
behaviour: and when I get a country place and a leisure hour shall
buckle to Uncle Tom and really try to read it.

Thackeray's essays on the horror of capital punishment
voiced his personal distress and did not carry him into public
action in support of abolition. Perhaps it was of himself he
spoke when he gave Henry Esmond the lines: "I can't but
accept the world as I find it, including a rope's end, as long
as it is in fashion." Dickens, Thackeray's great rival, was

much more committed to social reform and participated several years after the publication of Thackeray's essays in the campaigns to abolish capital punishment and public hangings. But certain points must be noted in Thackeray's favor. Dickens, in Philip Collins's words, was not "a masculine Madame Defarge," but he attended at least three, and possibly four, executions. Thackeray, though drawn powerfully by the fascination of public hanging, could bring himself, so far as we know, to attend only one execution and then he could not bear to look. While in Cairo in 1844 he declined an invitation to attend a public execution. He later explained his refusal in his *Journey from Cornhill to Grand Cairo* (1846): "Seeing one man hanged is quite enough in the course of a life. *J'y ai été*, as the Frenchman said of hunting."

Dickens, only a few years after ardent campaigning for total abolition of capital punishment, abandoned this position, though he remained convinced that hanging should not be conducted in public. It is doubtful that Thackeray ever qualified his beliefs, based as they were on the repugnance his flesh felt to the hanging of Courvoisier. His cousin Richard Bedingfield reports that Thackeray once deprecated his compliment on "Going to See a Man Hanged" with the remark: "I think I was wrong. My feelings were overwrought. These murderers are such devils, after all." But Bedingfield immediately adds after his recollection of this conversation that Thackeray "did not like the idea of capital punishment."

It is ironic that Lewis Melville, one of Thackeray's earlier biographers, cites this Bedingfield passage as a basis for inferring that Thackeray's views on capital punishment changed. It is Bedingfield who, among Thackeray's intimates, most clearly saw the link that bound his hatred of hanging to his ardent anti-evangelicalism and his loathing for bullies. Bedingfield writes elsewhere in his reminiscences of Thackeray:

He hated "Jack Ketch" and his worse than "bloody trade"; he hated all things unmerciful and ruthless. He sees "no hint of damning in the universe"; he inveighs against the lash in the army; he has a loathing detestation of bullies, small and big. . . .

No doubt the world is right in honoring those who struggle for just causes on the basis of intellectual or ideological conviction. But honor is also owed to those men like Thackeray, who, out of the sensitivity and responses of their own bodies and personalities, produce a cry of anguish which can move their fellow men to remember their humanity.

CHAPTER FOUR

The Mystery of Edwin Drood

The title of *Edwin Drood* advertises the book as a "mystery" novel. It is unfortunate that Dickens died when the book was only half completed, leaving no notes or sketches indicating how the balance of the story would proceed or what the conclusion was to be. In the century that has followed Dickens's death, literally hundreds of scholars and commentators have lavished a good deal of time and ingenuity in trying to establish, first of all, just where the "mystery" of *Edwin Drood* was intended to lie, and then to propose solutions for the various puzzles they found in the plot.

Dickens himself indicated to his friend and biographer, Forster, that there was to be something unique about the story. He said that he had "a very curious and new idea for my new story. Not a communicable idea (or the interest of the book would be gone), but a very strong one, though difficult to work."

In the orthodox modern detective novel, we expect the story to begin with a description of the circumstances that lead to the murder and constitute the puzzle the detective is to unravel. In the inverted detective story or crime novel, we are introduced to the intended murderer, taken (often pretty promptly) into his confidence about his murder plans, and then permitted to watch both the commission of the crime and the detection.

The Mystery of Edwin Drood begins in neither of these ways—it begins with a nightmare, an opium dream of John Jasper, at once lay precentor and choirmaster of Cloisterham Cathedral and a secret drug addict:

An ancient English Cathedral Tower? How can the ancient English Cathedral tower be here! The well known massive gray square tower of its old Cathedral? How can that be here! There is no spike of rusty iron in the air, between the eye and it, from any point of the real prospect. What is the spike that intervenes, and who has set it up? Maybe it is set up by the Sultan's orders for the impaling of a horde of Turkish robbers, one by one. It is so, for cymbals clash, and the Sultan goes by to his palace in long procession. Ten thousand scimitars flash in the sunlight, and thrice ten thousand dancing-girls strew flowers. Then follow white elephants caparisoned in countless gorgeous colours, and infinite in number and attendants. Still the Cathedral Tower rises in the background, where it cannot be, and still no writhing figure is on the grim spike. Stay! Is the spike so low a thing as the rusty spike on the top of a post of an old bedstead that has tumbled all awry? Some vague period of drowsy laughter must be devoted to the consideration of this possibility.

Shaking from head to foot, the man whose scattered consciousness has thus fantastically pieced itself together, at length rises, supports his trembling frame upon his arms, and looks around.

After the dreamer awakes (his identity not yet revealed), he hurries back to Cloisterham Cathedral in time for afternoon services. With Jasper's nightmare as prologue, the action begins.

John Jasper thus is met in the very first pages of the book. The principal characters are introduced quickly and the plot develops at a forced march. Jasper's nephew, Edwin Drood, was in infancy betrothed by his parents to Rosa Bud. The two are fond of each other, but not in love. Jasper, who teaches Rosa music, is, on the other hand, passionately in love with her. His feelings for Edwin appear to be a mixture of love and of jealousy over Edwin's tie with Rosa. Jasper appears to plot against Edwin, first stirring up bad blood between him and Neville Landless, who, with his sister Helena, has come from Ceylon to reside in Cloisterham under the care of Canon

Crisparkle. Jasper also begins to behave strangely, and among his most unusual actions is a nocturnal expedition he makes with the tombstone mason, Durdles, through the tower and crypt of the Cloisterham Cathedral. Shortly after this, Edwin (having in the meantime, unbeknownst to Jasper, broken off his engagement) disappears without a trace, except for certain jewelry later found by Canon Crisparkle in a weir on a river near Cloisterham. The balance of the *Drood* fragment includes an account of the persecution by Jasper of Neville Landless (who has also fallen in love with Rosa) for the "murder" of Drood; the arrival in Cloisterham of one Datchery, who is apparently a detective in disguise and maintains a watch over Jasper's actions; and the pursuit of Jasper by the Opium Woman, in whose den he dreamed the opium dream that served as the book's prologue and is to dream another dream, apparently describing a past act of violence.

This far the fragment takes us and no farther. In the story most *Drood* critics have fastened upon the following "mysteries":

Did John Jasper murder or attempt to murder Edwin Drood? Here there are subsidiary questions as to the place and manner of the crime and the eventual mode of detection.

Was Edwin dead or did he escape?

Who was Dick Datchery, the disguised detective?

Who was the Opium Woman?

As to the first question, almost all critics are in agreement that John Jasper either murdered or attempted to murder Edwin Drood. An exception is Felix Aylmer. It is Aylmer's theory (put forward in *The Drood Case*, published in 1965) that Jasper killed a man in Cloisterham—though the victim was not Edwin Drood, but a Moslem enemy seeking to murder Drood to avenge an ancient family feud—and that this killing occurred not on the Christmas Eve of Drood's disappearance but on the Christmas Eve of the year before. Ac-

cording to Aylmer, Jasper's famous nocturnal visit to the
cathedral was made not in preparation for Drood's murder,
but to attempt to reconstruct the earlier killing and to determine whether it was intentional or accidental. However, Aylmer's attempt to make a virtuous man out of Jasper runs into
difficult obstacles, including Jasper's brutal treatment of Rosa
Bud; and he appears to have written a new *Edwin Drood,*
much inferior to Dickens's.

More controversial is the question whether Edwin was
dead or whether (as most believers in his survival—with due
respect to Mr Aylmer—would have it) he survived a murderous assault by his uncle.

Among the leading exponents of the survival theory are
Andrew Lang and R. A. Proctor. Proctor believed that Drood
was the disguised Datchery, who was watching over Jasper
and awaiting an appropriate hour of vengeance. In his article
"Watched by the Dead" Proctor pointed to the pervasive-
ness in Dickens's writing of the theme of the criminal
watched, sometimes by one he thought to be dead. Proctor
also relied on a highly subjective feeling that the "music" of
the writing did not suggest that Edwin Drood was doomed
to die. Subjectiveness is, unfortunately, an occupational failing of Drood critics. Thus Mr. Aylmer thinks he sees an evolu-
tion of Jasper, between the preliminary sketches of Charles
Collins and the final illustrations of Luke Fildes, into a "hero
who looks like a villain."

Among the original evidence that has been relied on to
support the survival theory are certain alternative titles
listed by Dickens in his private notes on the book, namely:
"The Disappearance of Edwin Drood," "Edwin Drood in
Hiding" and "Dead? or Alive?" However, these alternatives
may indicate only that Dickens intended the ultimate fate of
Drood to remain unknown until the end, a purpose that was
served by the use of the noncommittal word "mystery" in the
title he decided upon. (Dickens as editor suggested on one
occasion to the author of a murder story the use of "mystery"

in the title to keep the fact of murder concealed.)

Another piece of evidence cited to prove Drood's survival is the middle picture at the bottom of Collins's sketch for the Drood cover, later elaborated in the final cover drawing by Fildes, who took over as illustrator. The "survivalists" say that this sketch shows Edwin Drood confronting John Jasper at the tomb of quicklime in which Jasper believed he had buried Drood's dead body. But interpreters of a contrary mind have said the sketch represents a hallucinatory image of the dead Drood summoned up by the guilty conscience of John Jasper. Others have said that Helena Landless appears in the drawing disguised as the dead Edwin.

The list of those who say that Edwin is dead is long and impressive. John Forster and Charles Dickens, Jr., have said that Dickens told them so. Luke Fildes claimed that Dickens informed him that Jasper was to strangle Edwin with Jasper's black scarf, which was to appear in the illustrations; Dickens had also intended to take Fildes to Maidstone Gaol to sketch the condemned cell, apparently as a basis for a drawing of Jasper in prison.

Among the critics, J. Cuming Walters and Edmund Wilson concluded that Drood was murdered. Some critics have drawn support for this conclusion from Dickens's notes for the completed chapters. The notes for an early chapter describing an interview between Drood and Jasper read ". . . murder far off"; those for the chapter describing Jasper's nighttime expedition through Cloisterham Cathedral include the phrase: "Lay the ground for the manner of the murder to come out at last." Many critics have interpreted the expedition either as a rehearsal of the eventual murder or as providing Jasper the means of obtaining a key to a tomb for the burial of Edwin's body as well as scouting the cathedral and its precincts as an intended site for the crime and disposition of the body.

What we might call quasi-judicial confirmation of the death of Edwin is provided by the manslaughter verdict returned by a blue-ribbon literary jury in a mock trial of John Jasper held in London in January 1914. The prosecutor was J. Cuming Walters. Justice Gilbert Keith Chesterton presided, and a certain G. Bernard Shaw served as foreman of the jury. The verdict was announced by Shaw:

MY LORD,—I am happy to be able to announce to your Lordship that we, following the tradition and practice of British Juries, have arranged our verdict in the luncheon interval. I should explain, my Lord, that it undoubtedly presented itself to us as a point of extraordinary difficulty in this case, that a man should disappear absolutely and completely, having cut off all communication with his friends in Cloisterham; but having seen and heard the society and conversation of Cloisterham here in Court to-day, we no longer feel the slightest surprise at that. Now, under the influence of that observation, my Lord, the more extreme characters, if they will allow me to say so, in this Jury, were at first inclined to find a verdict of Not Guilty, because there was no evidence of a murder having been committed; but on the other hand, the calmer and more judicious spirits among us felt that to allow a man who had committed a cold-blooded murder of which his own nephew was the victim, to leave the dock absolutely unpunished, was a proceeding which would probably lead to our all being murdered in our beds. And so you will be glad to learn that the spirit of compromise and moderation prevailed, and we find the prisoner guilty of Manslaughter.

We recommend him most earnestly to your Lordship's mercy, whilst at the same time begging your Lordship to remember that the protection of the lives of the community is in your hands, and begging you not to allow any sentimental consideration to deter you from applying the law in its utmost vigour.

Many efforts have been made to prove or disprove Edwin's death and the other principal mysteries of the fragment from clues left by Dickens in the book. Though these efforts are often ingenious, they fail to carry conviction. Mystery novels are not exercises in logic, but romances made to appear logical retrospectively. Dickens, like the great army of detective-story writers, good and bad, who have followed in his footsteps, scattered a great number of clues across his pages, some of which would prove to lead to the solution and others to lead nowhere. The essential arbitrariness of the mystery story has been brilliantly established in our own time by the interesting British crime novelist Anthony Berkeley. Having scored a great success with his short story about a poisoning, entitled "The Avenging Chance," he expanded it into a novel to which he gave the name *The Poisoned Chocolates Case*. In the novel, the facts of the crime are considered by a panel of six amateur detectives. Each detective, on the basis of an analogy to his own favorite historic poisoning case, reaches a different conclusion. The fifth comes to the conclusion Berkeley reached in the original short story. Then, as the final turn of the screw, the last detective arrives at the "correct" conclusion, one that is completely different from the short story's denouement.

The range of plot devices, now familiar from detective fiction, that were available to Dickens in concluding his tale may be illustrated by the problem of the identity of the disguised detective, Datchery. This problem is often closely related to the problem of the fate of Edwin, for, as has been mentioned, some of the believers in his survival identify Datchery with Drood entering into a vengeful watch over his attempted murderer. Most critics, regardless of their views as to Edwin's fate, agree that Datchery is a member of the group centering around the Landlesses, Rosa and their lawyer friend, Hiram Grewgious, who are suspicious of Jasper's involvement in Edwin's disappearance. All members of this group may roughly be said to have had, in crime-fiction parlance, the "opportunity" to assume the role of Datchery. There are substantial problems of time and place for all of them, but none that might not have been cured by quick trips between London and Cloisterham, in the manner of the closely-worked-out timetable dear to the hearts of Freeman Wills Crofts and his Inspector French. If Dickens, in choosing a character for the so-called Datchery assumption, was using the now-familiar device of the "least likely person," he might, as Felix Aylmer asserts he did, have chosen for this role Grewgious's apparently insignificant clerk, Bazzard. On the other hand, Dickens's choice for Datchery might have fallen, as Walters, Wilson and others contend, on Helena Landless, if he was relying on the famous plot device whereby the apparently least relevant fact becomes the most relevant. We are told early in the fragment that Helena has a talent for male disguise, having as a child run away from home disguised as a boy. But even here we are on dangerous ground, because others have argued that Helena's talent for disguise would be shown by her impersonation of the ghost of Edwin Drood in an attempt to frighten Jasper into incriminating himself.

Dickens left himself an even greater range of choices for the ultimate revelation of the identity of the Opium Woman and her motives for pursuing Jasper. Nobody among the cast of characters appears to know her, and Dickens was free to give her any personality and relationship he saw fit. Here Drood critics have given their imagination free rein, depicting her alternately as Jasper's mother or the mother of a girl he had wronged and later abandoned because of his mad infatuation with Rosa. Richard Baker concludes more prosaically that she was a blackmailer.

To my mind, the most interesting commentators have been those who conclude that though Dickens intended and successfully contrived to construct a baffling plot, the heart of the mystery was intended to lie not in the fate of Edwin or in the details of the crime and its detection, but in the psychology of Jasper and his eventual confrontation of his own misdeed. Forster states that Dickens told him:

the originality . . . was to consist in the review of the murderer's career by himself at the close, when its temptations were to be dwelt upon as if, not he the culprit, but some other man, were the tempted. The last chapters were to be written in the condemned cell, to which his wickedness, all elaborately elicited from him as if told of another, had brought him.

To this statement I would be audacious enough to add that the originality may have consisted also in showing the reader the genesis of a crime out of Jasper's opium-ridden psyche, and the motivation and preparation for the murder, while withholding for the end the details of its commission and its aftermath, and at the same time, confirmation for the reader's suspicion of Jasper's guilt.

Dickens's daughter, Kate Perugini, accepted Forster's account and added interesting comments of her own:

If those who are interested in the subject will carefully read what I have quoted, they will not be able to detect any word or hint from my father that it was upon the Mystery alone that he relied for the interest and originality of his idea. The originality was to be shown, as he tells us, in what we may call the psychological description the murderer gives us of his temptations, temperament, and character, as if told by another. . . . I do not mean to imply that the mystery itself had no strong hold on my father's imagination; but, greatly as he was interested in the intricacies of that tangled skein, the information he voluntarily gave to Mr. Forster, from whom he had withheld nothing for thirty-three years, certainly points to the fact that he was quite as deeply fascinated and absorbed in the study of the criminal Jasper, as in the dark and sinister crime that has given the book its title. . . . It was not, I imagine, for the intricate working out of his plot alone that my father cared to write this story; but it was through his wonderful observation of character, and his strange insight into the tragic secrets of the human heart, that he desired his greatest triumph to be achieved.

It has been left for more modern critics to elaborate the psychological significance of Jasper's crime. For Edmund Wilson, Jasper represents, like Raskolnikov, the duality of man and his innate simultaneous capacity for good and evil. Jasper lives in the respectable milieu of Victorian society and at the same time is what today we might call a "drop out"; he is a dope addict and a brutal murderer. I am reminded in this connection of the murder trial in 1879 (nine years after Dickens's death) of Charlie Peace, sometimes the respectable householder and, sometimes a highly competent burglar, and am reminded also of his eighteenth-century predecessor Deacon Brodie, who, as I have noted in an earlier chapter, served as the model for Stevenson's Dr. Jekyll and Mr. Hyde.

Edmund Wilson has also suggested certain surprising relationships between Jasper and Dickens himself. Dickens, the respectable Victorian, also lived the wilder life of imagination. He was so obsessed by murder that he continued to act out Bill Sikes's murder of Nancy at his public readings, despite the warnings of his tour manager, Dolby, that the passion he gave the piece was bad for his health. And further, Wilson suggests that Jasper's murder of a loved relative may have served subconsciously as an analogue to Dickens's sacrifice of his family duty to his love for Ellen Ternan.

Edgar Johnson, Dickens's modern biographer, has also underscored the social significance of Jasper's crime. For him the book is not only a detective story or the analysis of a criminal personality, but also a bitter indictment of the rotting society of Cloisterham (which has been identified as Dickens's home town, Rochester). To Johnson, Cloisterham stands as a symbol of the Victorian society, against which Jasper's crime and his whole life constituted a revolt. He points to the smugness and suffocating closeness of Cloisterham; the imperialistic feeling of superiority displayed by its good people, including Edwin, against foreigners (represented by the Landlesses); and the insincerity of bombastic philanthropy embodied in the unforgettable Mr. Honeythunder.

When these psychological and social implications are considered together with the admirable complexity of the plot, it is difficult to escape what is perhaps the only conclusion about the book that is beyond controversy: that *Edwin Drood*, if completed, would have been one of Dickens's greatest novels.

CHAPTER FIVE

Salieri and the "Murder" of Mozart

On October 14, 1791, in his last surviving letter, Mozart wrote to his wife, Constanze, at Baden that he had taken the Italian composer Antonio Salieri and the singer Madame Cavalieri to a performance of *The Magic Flute*, and that Salieri had been most complimentary: "from the overture to the last chorus there was not a single number that did not call forth from him a bravo! or bello!" Less than two months later, Mozart was dead. The *Musikalisches Wochenblatt*, in a report from Prague written within a week of the composer's death, mentioned rumors of poisoning based on the swollen condition of his body. Suspicion was gradually to focus on Salieri, who, despite his recently professed delight over *The Magic Flute*, had for a decade been an implacable rival of Mozart in Vienna. In the years prior to Salieri's death in 1825 the rumors of his recourse to poison as a final weapon of rivalry were fed by reports that Salieri, while in failing health, had confessed his guilt and, in remorse, had attempted suicide.

The rumors that Mozart was murdered and that Salieri was his assassin have produced controversies and traditions in the fields of medicine, musicology, history and literature which have not lost their vigor today. In 1970 a novel by David Weiss, entitled *The Assassination of Mozart*, appeared in the

63

bookshops. Medical and historical debate on Mozart's untimely demise continues both in this country and abroad, and German writers and researchers in particular show a remarkable preoccupation with the composer's death. The writings on this fascinating subject differ widely in quality and point of view, and many of the authors seem unaware of the sources on which others have drawn. It therefore remains tempting to return to this classic historical mystery with a view to providing a "confrontation" among the various contending parties, including those who blame Mozart's death, respectively, on natural causes, poisoning, professional jealousy, Viennese politics, the Masons and the Jews. In this centuries-long debate no possible suspect is spared. Virtually no organ of Mozart's body is regarded as above the suspicion of having failed in its appointed function, and with the exception of the composer's wife, no group or individual is cleared of complicity in his death.

The story of Mozart's last days must begin with the mysterious commissioning of the Requiem, which apparently caused his sensitive spirits to brood upon death. Around July of 1791, when Mozart's work on *The Magic Flute* was virtually complete and rehearsals had already begun, Mozart received a visit from a tall, grave-looking stranger dressed completely in gray. The stranger presented an anonymous letter commissioning Mozart to compose a Requiem as quickly as possible at whatever price the composer wished to name. It is now accepted that the commission had a very prosaic explanation. The patron of the uncanny-looking messenger was Count Franz von Walsegg, who wanted the Requiem composed in memory of his late wife, and intended to pass himself off as the composer. Mozart accepted the commission, but put aside his work on the Requiem when he received an offer to write an opera, *La Clemenza di Tito,* for the coronation of Emperor Leopold in Prague. Just as Mozart and his wife were getting into the coach to leave for Prague, the messenger appeared, it is said, "like a ghost" and pulled at

Constanze's coat, asking her, "What about the Requiem?" Mozart explained his reason for the journey, but promised to turn to the Requiem as soon as he came back to Vienna.

Franz Niemetschek, Mozart's first biographer, reports that Mozart became ill in Prague and required continuous medical attention while he was there. He states that Mozart "was pale and his expression was sad, although his good humour was often shown in merry jest with his friends."

On Mozart's return to Vienna, he started work on the Requiem with great energy and interest, but his family and friends noted that his illness was becoming worse and that he was depressed. To cheer him up, Constanze went driving with him one day in the Prater. According to her account, which she gave to Niemetschek, "Mozart began to speak of death, and declared that he was writing the Requiem for himself. Tears came to the eyes of this sensitive man. 'I feel definitely,' he continued, 'that I will not last much longer; I am sure I have been poisoned. I cannot rid myself of this idea.' " This conversation, which is one of the cornerstones of the poisoning legend, Constanze later repeated to her second husband, Georg Nikolaus von Nissen, who recorded it in his biography of Mozart in much the same terms as the Niemetschek version. Constanze was still recounting the episode as late as 1829, according to the journal of Vincent and Mary Novello, who paid her a visit in Salzburg that year. In fact, the Novellos' journal records that Constanze told them Mozart had clearly identified the poison that he thought had been administered to him as *aqua toffana*. This poison, whose principal active ingredient is supposed to have been arsenic, was introduced by a Neapolitan woman named Toffana in seventeenth-century Italy, with startling effect on the statistics of sudden death. It is perhaps regrettable that history has not seen fit to choose the most sublime of her various nicknames for the potion, the "manna of St. Nicholas di Bari."

One of the most dependable accounts of Mozart's terminal

illness is provided by Constanze's sister, Sophie Haibel, in a report sent in 1825 to Nissen at his request for use in his biography. Most of the symptoms with which the medical historians have dealt we owe to her account: the painful swelling of his body, which made it difficult for him to move in bed; his complaint that he had "the taste of death" on his tongue; his high fever. Despite his suffering, he continued to work on the Requiem. On the last day of the composer's life, when Sophie came to see him, Süssmayr was at his bedside and Mozart was explaining to him how he ought to finish the Requiem. (It is reported by a newspaper article contemporaneous with Sophie's memoir that earlier on this day Mozart was singing the alto part of the Requiem with three friends, who supplied falsetto, tenor and bass.) Mozart retained his worldly concerns to the point of advising Constanze to keep his death secret until his friend Albrechtsberger could be informed, so that his friend could make prompt arrangements to succeed to Mozart's recently granted rights as colleague and heir apparent of the Kapellmeister of St. Stephen's Cathedral. When Mozart appeared to be sinking, one of his doctors, Nikolaus Closset, was sent for and was finally located at the theater. However, according to Sophie's account, that drama-lover "had to wait till the piece was over." When he arrived, he ordered cold compresses put on Mozart's feverish brow, but these "provided such a shock that he did not regain consciousness again before he died." The last thing Mozart did, according to Sophie, was to imitate the kettledrums in the Requiem. She wrote that thirty-four years later she could still hear that last music of his.

Nissen, in his biography, states that Mozart's fatal illness lasted for fifteen days, terminating with his death around midnight (probably the early morning) of December 5, 1791. The illness began with swellings of his hands and feet and an almost complete immobility, and sudden attacks of vomiting followed. Nissen describes the illness as "high miliary fever." He writes that Mozart retained consciousness until two hours before his death.

Neither Dr. Closset nor Mozart's other attending physician prepared a death certificate with the cause of death stated. No autopsy was performed. From the very beginning, doctors and other commentators have differed widely as to the cause of death. Nissen's identification of the fatal illness as "miliary fever" accords with the cause of death as set forth in the registers of deaths of St. Stephen's Cathedral and Parish in Vienna. Although that nomenclature does not fit any precise modern medical definition, it is surmised that the term as used in the medicine of the eighteenth century denoted a fever accompanied by a rash. However, a number of other illnesses have been put forward as the cause of death, including grippe, tuberculosis, dropsy, meningitis, rheumatic fever, heart failure and Graves' disease. The hypotheses of some of these diseases, such as tuberculosis, appear to have been based not so much on any of the observable medical phenomena as on a biographical conclusion that Mozart in his last years was killing himself with overwork and irregular living. The hypothesis of Graves' disease, a hyperthyroidism, is based on facial characteristics of Joseph Lange's unfinished 1782 portrait of the composer, which include, in the words of an imaginative medical observer, "the wide angle of the eye, the staring, rather frightened look, the swelling of the upper eyelid and the moist glaze of the eyes." The art historian Kenneth Clark has quite a different interpretation of Mozart's intent gaze in the Lange portrait. The painting conveys to Lord Clark not the sign of death nine years off, but "the single-mindedness of genius."

Probably the prevailing theory of modern medical authorities who believe Mozart to have died a natural death is that he suffered from a chronic kidney disease, which passed in its final stages into a failure of kidney function, edema (swelling due to excessive retention of liquid in the body tissues) and uremic poisoning. This theory was advanced as early as 1905 by a French physician, Dr. Barraud. It is argued that this diagnosis is most in keeping with the recorded phenomena of Mozart's last sufferings, including the swelling of his body and the poisonous taste of which he complained. Modern medicine has established that certain chronic diseases of the kidneys are commonly caused by streptococcal infections suffered long before the effect on the kidney function becomes noticeable.

Medical commentators on Mozart's death have implicated a number of childhood illnesses as likely contributors to his chronic kidney disease. They are aided in their researches by detailed descriptions of the illnesses of the Mozart children in the letters of their father, Leopold. Certainly their recurring health problems were a proper subject of parental concern, but the pains Leopold takes to describe his children's symptoms and the course of their illnesses and recoveries stamp him as an amateur of medicine. In fact, he often administered remedies to the children, his favorites being a carthartic and an antiperspirant he refers to as "black powder" and "margrave powder," respectively. It is fortunate that the children survived both a series of diseases and their father's cures.

In 1762, when Wolfgang was six years old, he was ill with what a doctor consulted by Leopold Mozart declared to be a type of scarlet fever, an infection capable of causing kidney injury. In the following year, 1763, Mozart suffered an illness marked by painful joints and fever, which have led some observers to postulate rheumatic fever, which could also lead to adverse effects on the kidney. When Mozart was nine he suffered from what Leopold called a "very bad cold," and later the same year both his sister and he were more seriously ill. Nannerl was thought to be in such serious condition that the administration of extreme unction was begun. No sooner had she recovered than Wolfgang was struck by the illness, which in his father's words reduced him in a period of four weeks to such a wretched state that "he is not only absolutely unrecognizable, but has nothing left but his tender skin and little bones." Some modern commentators identify this severe illness as an attack of abdominal typhus. Two years later, in 1767, Wolfgang contracted smallpox, which left him quite ill and caused severe swelling of his eyes and nose. He also suffered throughout his childhood from a number of bad toothaches, which have led some supporters of the kidney-disease theory to invoke the possibility of a "focal" infection, contributing to kidney damage. The last reference to an illness of Mozart prior to his final days is in a letter from Leopold Mozart to his daughter Nannerl in 1784, when her brother was twenty-eight. This letter reported that Wolfgang had become violently ill with colic in Vienna and had a doctor in almost daily attendance. Leopold added that not only his son, "but a number of other people caught rheumatic fever, which became septic when not taken in hand at once." There is no other evidence of a serious illness of Mozart's until the period of a few months preceding his death. Dr. Louis Carp attempts to demonstrate the presence of severe symptoms of kidney disease as early as 1787 by quoting from a letter of Mozart to his father in April of that year: "I never lie down at night without reflecting that—young as I am—I may not live to see another day." This letter, written to console Mozart's dying father, gives us an important insight into the composer's metaphysical speculations. However, it does not provide any clue to his own physical condition or to his feelings about his health.

Locked in interesting combat with the medical authorities attributing Mozart's death to disease is a substantial body of modern physicians who would support Mozart's own suspicion by declaring that he was indeed poisoned. These doctors, including Dieter Kerner and Gunther Duda of Germany, believe that the poison administered was mercury, which attacks the kidneys and produces much the same diagnostic picture as that presented by the final stages of a natural kidney failure. Both Kerner and Duda minimize much of the evidence that has been cited in support of the theory that Mozart suffered from a chronic kidney disease stemming from streptococcal infection. Dr. Duda believes that the severity and nature of Mozart's childhood illnesses have been misstated. He is convinced that the so-called scarlet fever identified as such by the physician whom Mozart's father consulted was, in fact, erythema nodosum, a disorder of uncertain origin resulting in raised eruptions of the skin, and of far less severity than scarlet fever. Moreover, Duda is not at all certain that other illnesses of Mozart's, which have been identified as rheumatic fever, were not, instead, common cases of the grippe. He is unimpressed by the speculation that Mozart's toothaches may have involved harmful focal infections. He points out that Mozart's sister, who was exposed to and suffered most of the same childhood illnesses as Mozart, lived to the age of seventy-eight, and finds no evidence that Mozart himself had any substantial illness between 1784 and the last year of his life.

Dr. Kerner believes that the phenomena of Mozart's last illness more closely resemble those of mercury poisoning than of the last stages of a chronic kidney illness. He notes the absence of any evidence that Mozart complained of thirst, which Dr. Kerner associates with chronic nephritis. He also notes that Mozart was working actively to the last and was fully conscious, composing, during the last few months of his life, some of his greatest masterpieces. In contrast with this spectacular creative activity, it is Dr. Kerner's experience that "uremics are always for weeks and usually months before their death unable to work and for days before their death are unconscious." Dr. Kerner accepts the contemporary report that Mozart first became ill in Prague, and assumes that small doses of mercury were given to him in the summer of 1791, followed by a lethal dose shortly before his death. Dr. Kerner alludes to the fact that in the Vienna of Mozart's time mercury was in limited use as a remedy for syphilis and states that such use was introduced by Dr. Gerhard van Swieten, whose son Mozart knew. From such observations a recent commentator has erroneously read Dr. Kerner as arguing that Mozart poisoned himself in an effort to cure himself of syphilis.

It is hard for a modern reader of these arguments to rid himself of the prejudice against regarding a poisoning as anything but an exotic possibility. Unfortunately, it was for good experiential reasons not so regarded in the eighteenth century. Duda, in an effort to prepare his readers to accept his thesis, begins his book with the reminder that before firearms became generally available, poison was an extremely common weapon, and the subtle arts of its use well known. It is remarkable how many of Mozart's contemporaries who figure in some manner in the controversies over his death regarded poisoning or suspicion of poisoning as risks to be taken quite seriously.

Even if the medical evidence and eighteenth-century experience do not exclude the poisoning of Mozart as a possibility, there has always been difficulty in identifying a murderer and finding an appropriate murder motive. Salieri has always been the prime candidate for the unhappy role of Mozart's murderer. He fits this assignment imperfectly at best. Although (in large part due to the effect of the murder legend) time has not been kind to Salieri's musical reputation, he was undoubtedly one of the leading composers of his period and an important teacher of composition, counting among his pupils Beethoven, Schubert, Liszt, Hummel, Süssmayr, Sechter, and Meyerbeer. He was also a famous teacher of singing. All his students loved and respected him. Friends remembered him as generous, warm and kind-hearted, and he even had the ability to laugh at himself (at least at his difficulties with the German language). He must have had a way with people, since he apparently established a close personal relationship with the difficult Beethoven.

However, the musicians whose careers Salieri helped to forward shared an advantage that Mozart lacked—they all had the good fortune not to be competitors of Salieri in the composition of Italian opera. There seems little question but that he was a formidable professional opponent of Mozart, although they appear to have been able to sustain correct and even superficially friendly social relationships. Salieri enjoyed a competitive supremacy over Mozart and many other aspiring composers in Vienna, and only partly because of the undoubtedly high regard in which his contemporaries held Salieri's own operatic works. Of far greater importance in his ascendancy was the fact that, because of his favor with Joseph II until the emperor's death in 1790 and of his successive roles as court composer, director of the Italian Opera and court conductor, Salieri was able to wield powerful influence over the availability of theaters and patronage. Mozart, his father and many of their contemporaries believed that Salieri had caused the emperor to be unfavorably disposed toward *The Abduction from the Seraglio,* and had also been responsible for the later plot (fortunately unsuccessful) to induce the court to hamper the opening of *The Marriage of Figaro.* In his letters to his father, Mozart also accused Salieri of having prevented him from obtaining as a piano pupil the princess of Württemberg. In December 1789, Mozart wrote to his fellow Freemason and benefactor, Puchberg, that next time they met, he would tell him about Salieri's plots "which, however, have completely failed."

Although Mozart was undoubtedly very sensitive about barriers to his career, his feeling that Salieri used court influence to frustrate his musical competitors is borne out in the memoirs of Michael Kelly and Lorenzo da Ponte, who worked with both Mozart and Salieri and were on friendly terms with each. Kelly refers to Salieri as "a clever, shrewd man, possessed of what Bacon called crooked wisdom," and adds that Salieri's effort to have one of his operas selected for performance instead of *The Marriage of Figaro* was "backed by three of the principal performers, who formed a cabal not easily put down." Da Ponte blames attempts to disrupt rehearsals of *Figaro* on the opera impresario Count Orsini-Rosenberg and a rival librettist, Casti, rather than directly on Salieri, although both men appear to have been in Salieri's camp. He also remarks that before he came to the rescue, "Mozart had, thanks to the intrigues of his rivals, never been able to exercise his divine genius in Vienna." Da Ponte was a slippery man with an elastic memory; it is probably fair to attribute to him the assessment of Salieri that he claimed to have heard from the lips of Emperor Leopold: "I know all his intrigues . . . Salieri is an insufferable egoist. He wants successes in my theatre only for his own operas and his own women. . . . He is an enemy of all composers, all singers, all Italians; and above all, my enemy, because he knows that I know him."

Nevertheless, there is much to suggest that Salieri's hostility to Mozart did not extend to the sphere of personal relations. He was one of the small group of mourners who followed Mozart's coffin as it was carried from the funeral service at St. Stephen's Cathedral toward the cemetery, making a greater display of public grief over Mozart's death than Constanze, who stayed at home, supposedly still overcome by her husband's death. Moreover, Salieri later became the teacher of Mozart's son Franz Xaver Wolfgang and in 1807 gave him a written testimonial which procured him his first musical appointment.

It is difficult to decide whether Constanze or the Mozart family gave any credence to the rumors against Salieri. Would Constanze have entrusted the musical education of her son to a man she believed to be the murderer of his father? Nissen's biography contains an allusion to Salieri's rivalry, but rejects the poisoning charges. Nissen reports that Constanze attributed Mozart's suspicion of poisoning to illness and overwork. Moreover, he included in his biography an anonymous account of Mozart's early death which had been published in 1803. The quoted article dismisses the possibility of poisoning and attributes Mozart's fears to "pure imagination."

Nissen's biography was undoubtedly written and compiled with Constanze's blessing. However, as witnessed by her conversations with the Novellos, which took place at approximately the same time as the appearance of the biography,

Constanze never put Mozart's suspicions out of her mind. Her preoccupation with this subject reappears a decade later in a letter written to a Munich official (and quoted by Kerner in his study) to the effect that "her son Wolfgang Xaver knew that he would not, like his father, have to fear envious men who had designs on his life." Her other son, Karl, on his death in 1858 left behind, according to Kerner, a handwritten commentary, in which there is further discussion of the poisoning of Mozart—this time by a "vegetable poison."

The views of Mozart's contemporaries as to Salieri's guilt doubtlessly divided along lines of personal or musical loyalties. In the years 1823 through 1825 partisans of Salieri rallied to the defense of his reputation in the face of widely circulated reports that he had confessed the murder and attempted suicide by cutting his throat. When Kapellmeister, Schwanenberg, a friend of Salieri's, was read a newspaper account of the rumor that Mozart had fallen victim to Salieri's envy, he shouted, "Crazy people! He [Mozart] did nothing to deserve such an honor." But believers in the poisoning rumors were tireless and ingenious in spreading their gospel. At a performance of Beethoven's Ninth Symphony in Vienna on May 23, 1824, concertgoers were distributed a leaflet containing a poem which pictured Salieri as Mozart's rival "standing by his side with the poisoned cup." Giuseppe Carpani, a friend of Salieri and an early biographer of Haydn, responded with an effective public relations campaign in behalf of his maligned compatriot. He published a letter he had received in June 1824 from Dr. Guldener, who had not attended Mozart but had spoken to Mozart's physician, Dr. Closset. The latter had advised him, Guldener wrote, that Mozart's fatal illness had been a rheumatic and inflammatory fever which had attacked many people in Vienna in 1791. Dr. Guldener had added that in view of the large number of people who had seen Mozart during his illness and the experience and industry of Dr. Closset, "it could not have escaped their notice then if even the slightest trace of poisoning had

manifested itself." (Presumably Dr. Closset was quite indus-
trious after theater hours.) Carpani appended the text of
Guldener's letter to his own article defending Salieri's innocence. The Salieri press campaign also included a statement
by the two men who served as Salieri's keepers in his last
years of declining health. They attested that they had been
with him day and night and had never heard him confess the
murder.

The views of Beethoven on the poisoning rumors have
always been an intriguing subject because of his love of Mozart's music and his friendship with Salieri. We know from
the entries in his conversation books that Beethoven's callers
gossiped about the case with him. In late 1823 the publisher
Johann Schickh referred to Salieri's unsuccessful suicide attempt. In the following year Beethoven's nephew Karl and
his friend and future biographer, Anton Schindler, mentioned the reports of Salieri's confession of the poisoning, and
Karl, in May 1825, the month of Salieri's death, mentioned
the persistence of the rumors. It is generally agreed that
Beethoven did not believe Salieri guilty. He was fond of
referring to himself as Salieri's pupil, and after Mozart's
death he dedicated the violin sonatas Opus 12 to Salieri
(1797) and wrote a set of ten piano variations on a duet from
Salieri's charming opera *Falstaff* (1798). Nevertheless, wag-
ging tongues delighted in passing along a spurious anecdote
that Rossini, when he had induced Salieri to take him to visit
Beethoven at his Vienna home, was angrily turned away at
the door with the words: "How dare you come to my house
with Mozart's poisoner?"

The irony of the Beethoven-Rossini anecdote lies in the
fact that the lives of both men were touched by fears and
rumors of poisoning. Beethoven believed that his hated sister-in-law Johanna had poisoned his brother and intended to
poison his nephew. Rossini's mourning for the early death of
his friend Vincenzo Bellini in Paris was followed, as was Salieri's attendance at Mozart's funeral, by rumors of poisoning.

But the Bellini poisoning legend was cut down in its infancy as a result of decisive action on the part of Rossini. Francis Toye writes that "Rossini, unwilling, perhaps, to figure as a second Salieri, insisted on an autopsy, which put an end to the rumor once and for all."

It almost appears that Salieri was the only musical protagonist in the case who is not reported to have been subject to fears of poisoning. However, we have the intriguing biographical note that Salieri, though from a land of wine, drank only water. His modest drink, unlike headier beverages, would have given his taste buds early warning should an enemy have surreptitiously added a splash of *aqua toffana*.

Most of Mozart's principal biographers have either held aloof from the poisoning theory or rejected it outright. Franz Niemetschek, the first biographer (1798), appears to straddle the issue. Although he purported to blame lack of exercise and overwork for Mozart's death, he left room for a more sinister possibility: "These were probably the chief causes of his untimely death (if, in fact, it was not hastened unnaturally)." He also attributed Emperor Joseph's critical remarks about *The Abduction from the Seraglio* to "the cunning Italians" and added toward the conclusion of his work that "Mozart had enemies too, numerous, irreconcilable enemies, who pursued him even after his death." These enemies, including Salieri, were still alive, and Niemetschek, whatever his suspicions, could not very well have gone much further in pointing a finger.

Edward Holmes (1845) was the first to exonerate Salieri expressly. He relegated the poisoning legend to a footnote and concluded that "Salieri, the known inveterate foe of Mozart, was fixed upon as the imaginary criminal." Otto Jahn, in his great study of Mozart (1856–1859), continued to keep the charges of poisoning imprisoned in a footnote, and referred to the suspicions of Salieri's guilt as "shameful." Hermann Abert preserves Jahn's fleeting reference to the murder legend, and observes that Mozart's suspicion of poisoning evidenced his "morbidly overstimulated emotional state." Arthur Schurig blames Mozart's death on a severe grippe. Alfred Einstein not only fails to dignify the poisoning tradition by any mention, but even finds the only explanation for Salieri's animosity in Mozart's "wicked tongue." Eric Blom and Nicholas Slonimsky have rejected the possibility of murder, but have fortunately taken the trouble to chronicle some of the excesses of the various murder theories. However, both Russia and Germany have in our time produced writers who claim to have found "historical" evidence which not only supports the murder thesis but reveals a political motive for the crime and for the prevention of its detection.

The Soviet musicologist, Igor Boelza, in his brochure *Mozart and Salieri*, published in Moscow in 1953, exhibits a chain of hearsay evidence to the effect that Salieri's priest made a written report of his confession of the murder. He claims that the late Soviet academician Boris Asafiev told him that he had been shown the report by Guido Adler, also deceased. Boelza states that Adler had also spoken of the document to "colleagues and numerous scholars," none of whom is named in the brochure. According to Boelza, Adler engaged in a detailed study of the dates and circumstances of the meetings of Mozart and Salieri and established that they bore out the facts of the confession and satisfied the classic element of "opportunity." But Adler apparently was no more ready to publish his Inspector French–style timetable than he was willing to publish the Salieri confession itself. It is small wonder that Alexander Werth, in commenting on Boelza's book, remarks: "It looks as if the Adler mystery has taken the place of the Salieri mystery."

Boelza also seeks support for the murder case in the mysterious circumstances of Mozart's funeral and burial, which German writers like to refer to as *die Grabfrage* (the burial question). Posterity has always been puzzled by the fact that only a few friends (including Salieri) accompanied the funeral procession, and that even they turned back before arriving at the cemetery. The burial was that of a poor man and Mozart's body was placed in an unmarked grave. These bitter facts, so inappropriate to memorializing the passing of a great genius and a man who had loving friends and family, have been variously explained, and even the explanation least flattering to Mozart's circle usually falls short of implication of criminal conduct. Constanze's absence and the mourners' desertion before the cemetery gates have traditionally been blamed on a wintry storm, but this explanation is belied both by a contemporary diary and by an intelligent modern inquiry made by Nicolas Slonimsky of the Viennese weather archives. Nissen does not mention the weather in his biography and attributes Constanze's absence to her overpowering grief. The poverty of the burial has sometimes been taken to reflect the stinginess of Mozart's friends and patrons, notably of Baron van Swieten, though others have claimed that the burial was in keeping with the surviving spirit of decrees of Emperor Joseph II enacted in 1784 and repealed in the following year. These decrees, inspired by the reforming emperor's dislike for the pomp of burial, had provided that the dead not be buried in coffins but merely sewn in sacks and covered with quicklime, and had also abolished most of the funeral ceremonies.

In Boelza's version, all the events of Mozart's interment take on a more sinister significance. He conjures up a plot, headed by Baron van Swieten, and joined by all of the composer's acquaintances and relatives (with the exception of Constanze). On van Swieten's orders, all the mourners departed on the way to the grave and the body was intentionally interred in unmarked ground. In supplying a motive for this strange plot to suppress traces of the murder, Boelza brings the case into the political arena and adds a Marxist twist. It seems that van Swieten was afraid that "nationalist upheavals" would result if the working masses of imperialist Vienna learned of the report that Mozart had been poisoned by a court musician and, what was worse, by a foreigner.

German writers have produced a rival tradition that Mozart was murdered by his Freemason brethren. The Masonic
murder theory was apparently originated in 1861 by Georg
Friedrich Daumer, a researcher of antiquities and religious
polemicist. Daumer's work was elaborated in the Nazi period, notably by General Erich Ludendorff and his wife,
Mathilde, who were so fired by enthusiasm for their revelations that they devoted the family press to the propagation
of their indictment of the Freemasons.

The case against the Freemasons takes a number of lines.
Daumer claimed that Mozart had not fully carried out
Masonry's "party line" in *The Magic Flute*. Mozart, in his
view, had offended the Masons by his excessive attachment
to the figure of the Queen of the Night and by his use of
Christian religious music in the chorale of the Men of Armor.
Daumer also believed that the murder thwarted Mozart's
plan to establish his own secret lodge, to be called "The
Grotto." Mathilde Ludendorff built upon Daumer's imagin-
ings. She preferred, however, another explanation of the
Masons' outrage at *The Magic Flute*. She believed that Mozart had hidden under the pro-Masonic surface of the opera
a secret counterplot which depicted Mozart (Tamino) seeking the release of Marie Antoinette (Pamina) from her Masonic captors. Mathilde Ludendorff, like Igor Boelza, added
an element of nationalism. She claims that the murder was
also motivated by the opposition of the Freemasons to Mozart's hope of establishing a German opera theater in Vienna.
Both Daumer and Mathilde Ludendorff relate Mozart's
death to other murders of famous men in which they likewise
see the Masonic hand at work. Daumer's conviction of the
correctness of his view of Mozart's death was reinforced by
his belief that the Freemasons had also murdered Lessing,
Leopold II, and Gustav III of Sweden (who was murdered at
the famous masked ball only a few months after Mozart's
death). Mathilde Ludendorff expanded this list of victims to
include Schiller and, in a virtuoso display of freedom from

chronology, Martin Luther as well.

It is not surprising that the Ludendorff writings have a heavy overlay of anti-Semitism. General Ludendorff claimed that the secret of Masonry was the Jew and that its aim was to rob the Germans of their national pride and to assure the "glorious future of the Jewish people." He attempted to establish a Jewish role in Mozart's murder by the mysterious comment that Mozart had died "on the Day of Jehovah." The combination of anti-Semitic and anti-Masonic prejudices had been common since the nineteenth century and was intensified at the turn of the century in the heat of passions generated by the Dreyfus affair. It is ironic to observe this marriage of hates in retroactive operation in the Mozart case, since Masonic lodges of the eighteenth century generally excluded Jews from membership. There is reason to speculate, at least, that Mozart himself did not develop the racist insanity which so many of his countrymen have shown in later periods of history. Paul Nettl observes that if he had done so, the world would have lost the fruits of his collaboration with the talented Jewish librettist Lorenzo da Ponte. To be regarded as further evidence of Mozart's receptivity to the ideas of Jewish writers is the catalogue of his library of books left at his death, which lists a work on the immortality of the soul by Moses Mendelssohn.

The anti-Masonic murder theory, like the Boelza theory, assumes a conspiracy of Mozart's friends and family. Mathilde Ludendorff incriminates Salieri, van Swieten, and even the mysterious messenger who commissioned the Requiem. She accuses this oddly assorted group of slowly poisoning Mozart and of employing Nissen to cover up the crime in his biography. Constanze is, as a good and loyal housewife, spared any suggestion of complicity. However, as in Boelza's theory, her absence from the burial and its strange character are removed from the plane of personal and financial circumstance and explained by the conscious design of the conspirators. Frau Ludendorff even supplies the ghoulish hypothesis that the burial conformed to requirements of Masonry that the body of a transgressor against its laws must be denied decent burial.

Strangely enough, the Masonic murder legend has also been denied burial. Dr. Gunther Duda, whose medical views of the case have already been cited, is a "true believer" in the researches of Daumer and the Ludendorffs. His book *Gewiss, man hat mir Gift gegeben* ("I am sure I have been poisoned"), a comprehensive study of Mozart's death written in 1950, is prefaced with a quotation from Mathilde Ludendorff. He views the charges against the Masons as having been established with the same compelling force as a mathematical or logical formula. He supports the condemnation of the Masons by the following syllogism, all of the links in which he accepts as fact: (1) Mozart was a Mason; (2) the Masonic lodges claimed the right to sentence disobedient members to death; (3) Mozart was a disobedient member; and (4) the execution of the Masonic death sentence is evidenced by Mozart's death, the manner in which he died and the circumstances of his burial. However, Duda's zeal for his cause carries him well beyond the bounds of medical history or even plain logic. Faced with the question of why the Masons would not have punished not only Mozart but the librettists of *The Magic Flute* as well, he notes with suspicion the sudden deaths of the two men who may have collaborated on the libretto. The principal libretist, Emanuel Schikaneder, died in 1812 (twenty-one years after the opera's premiere), and Karl Ludwig Gieseke, who may also have had some role in shaping the libretto, died in 1833. Dr. Duda must surely be suggesting that the Freemasons had at their disposal the slowest poison in the annals of crime.

Dr. Kerner, in the 1967 edition of his study of Mozart's death, does not expressly join in the accusations against Freemasonry. However, his sober medical discussion passes at the end of his work into a vapor of astrology and symbolism which may enshroud suggestions of conspiracy. He points out that a "Hermes stele" pictured on the left side of an engraving on the frontispiece of the first libretto of *The Magic Flute* contains eight allegories of Mercury, the god who gave his name to the poison that Kerner believes killed Mozart. The engraving was made by the Freemason Ignaz Alberti. The allusion to Mercury in Alberti's frontispiece indicates to Kerner that more people were "in the know" about the murder than is generally assumed. He demonstrates the continuity of this secret knowledge over the centuries by observing that the special Mozart postage stamp issued by Austria in 1956 shows eight Mercury allegories in its frame. Dr. Kerner passes from iconography to alchemy and then to sinister hints. He states that in the symbolism of the alchemists the number 8 as well as the color gray represented the planet Mercury, "which reawakens lively associations of thought with the 'Gray Messenger,' who often put Mozart in fear in his last days."

Neither Dr. Duda nor Dr. Kerner attempts to reconcile with the Masonic murder theory their shared medical assumption that Mozart's poisoning began in the summer of 1791, before *The Magic Flute* was first performed. Moreover, if Mozart was out of favor with his Masonic brethren, a mind disinclined to conspiratorial thinking would find it hard to explain the commission he received shortly before his death to compose a Masonic cantata or the emotional oration that was delivered to a Masonic lodge in memory of Mozart and was printed in 1792 by the very same Freemason Alberti whose "Hermes stele" struck Kerner as suspicious.

The elements of conspiratorial thinking and exoticism have recently been supplied in abundant measure. Since the publication of their separate researches Drs. Kerner and Duda have, in collaboration with Dr. Johannes Dalchow, written two books which make more explicit their incrimination of the Masons as the murderers of Mozart. As elaborated in *Mozarts Tod* (1971), Masonry's involvement in Mozart's death was complex and premeditated. According to the authors (who in this respect as in many others parrot the writings of Mathilde Ludendorff), the "gray messenger" ordering the Requiem was not the agent of Count von Walsegg, but an emissary of the Masons announcing their death sentence. What was the reason for Mozart's murder? The authors provide two possibilities and like them both so well they do not choose between them: (1) a "ritual murder" in which Mozart was offered as a sacrifice to the Masonic deities; and (2) a punishment of Mozart by the Masons, with the participation of Salieri, for the crime of having revealed Masonic secrets in *The Magic Flute*. The authors engage in an extended numerological exegesis of *The Magic Flute* which is believed by them to prove the Masonic murder (and presumably also Mozart's acceptance of his execution). The authors assert that the number 18 is paramount in the music and libretto of the opera, by intentional association with the eighteenth "Rosicrucian" degree of Masonry, and that Mozart's death was also scheduled to give prominence to this number. It is observed with triumph by Dr. Kerner and his colleagues that Mozart's Masonic cantata was performed on November 18, 1791, exactly eighteen days before his death! Amid all this mystification the medical researches of the authors have come to play a minor role, and the bigoted spirit of Mathilde Ludendorff lives again.

The novelists have, since the very year of Salieri's death, had a field day with the theme of the poisoning. The succession of bad novels that stress the poisoning has continued unabated to our own day; certainly in the running for honors as the worst novel on the poisoning is David Weiss's *The Assassination of Mozart,* which summons up a vision (straight out of John Le Carré and Len Deighton) of a reactionary Austrian regime giving tacit approval to Salieri's murder of Mozart and ruthlessly suppressing every attempt to investigate the crime.

However, the poisoning tradition has produced one authentic masterpiece, Pushkin's short dramatic dialogue *Mo-*

zart and Salieri, conceived in 1826, only one year after Salieri's death, when the rumors of his confession were still in the air, and completed in 1830. In the Pushkin play (later set by Rimsky-Korsakov as an opera), Salieri poisons Mozart both because Mozart's superior gifts have made Salieri's lifelong devotion to music meaningless and because Mozart has introduced Salieri's soul to the bitterness of envy. Unlike many of Mozart's later admirers, Pushkin does not depict Salieri as a mediocre hack but rather as a dedicated musician who was intent on the perfection of his craft and was able to appreciate innovative genius (as in the case of his master, Gluck) and to assimilate it into his own development. However, Salieri refers to himself as a "priest" of music to whom his art is holy and serious. He is enraged by Mozart's free, creative spirit and by what he sees as Mozart's light-hearted, almost negligent, relation to the products of his genius. Salieri's assessment of his rival is confirmed for him by the joy Mozart takes in a dreadful performance of an air from *Figaro* by a blind fiddler. As was true in their real lives, both Salieri and Mozart in Pushkin's pages inhabit a world where poisoning is assumed to be a possible event even in the lives of famous and civilized men. Mozart refers to the rumor that "Beaumarchais once poisoned someone," and Salieri alludes to a tradition that Michelangelo murdered to provide a dead model for a Crucifixion. In Pushkin's version the murder of Mozart provides no relief for Salieri's torment, but only furnishes final proof of his inferiority. At the close of the play Salieri is haunted by Mozart's observation immediately before being poisoned that "genius and crime are two incompatible things."

Even if we suspect that the play has attributed to Salieri more subtlety as a criminal than he displayed in years of crude plotting against Mozart's musical career, Pushkin possibly comes closer to explaining how Salieri could have made a confession of guilt than does the inconclusive medical evidence or the references to Viennese court intrigue or Ma-

sonic plots. Salieri might have recognized the depth of the
animosity he had harbored. He might have come to the understanding that, if the essential life of a divinely gifted composer is in his art, he and others who had stood again and
again between Mozart and his public had, with malice afore-
thought, set out to "murder" Mozart. Pushkin's view of the
criminality of selfish opposition to artistic greatness is inci-
sively stated in a brief note written in 1832 on the origin of
the poisoning legend. Pushkin writes that at the premiere of
Don Giovanni the enthralled audience was shocked to hear
hissing and to see Salieri leaving the hall "in a frenzy and
consumed by envy." The note concludes: "The envious man
who was capable of hissing at *Don Giovanni* was capable of
poisoning its creator."

There is more reason to attribute to Salieri the symbolic
crime of attempted "murder" of a brother artist's work than
to speculate that Salieri was a poisoner. This judgment would
be supported by the testimony of Ignaz Moscheles. Moscheles, who was a former pupil of Salieri's and loved him
dearly, visited the old man in the hospital shortly before his
death. According to Moscheles's account, Salieri hinted at
the poisoning rumors and tearfully protested his innocence.
Although Moscheles wrote that he was greatly moved by the
interview and that he had never given the rumors the slightest belief, he added the following comment: "Morally speaking he [Salieri] had no doubt by his intrigues poisoned many
an hour of Mozart's existence." In his fictional account of the
Salieri protestation Bernard Grun attributes Moscheles's
comment about moral guilt to Salieri himself, thus harmoniz-
ing the interview with the rumors of Salieri's "confession."
According to the Novellos' journal, Mozart's son Franz Xaver
Wolfgang expressed a similar view, namely, that Salieri had
not murdered his father, but that "he may truly be said to
have poisoned his life and this thought . . . pressed upon the
wretched man when dying."

If Moscheles's narrative is accepted, many events become

easier to explain. Salieri's delight over *The Magic Flute* may have been genuine. It is possible that even in Mozart's lifetime Salieri finally acknowledged Mozart's genius and tempered his own feeling of rivalry. Tardy recognition of Mozart's greatness (and, perhaps, regret for their estrangement) may also account for Salieri's attendance at the funeral and his kindness to Mozart's son.

If Salieri was guilty of hostility to Mozart's art but not of poisoning, his punishment can only be called "cruel and unusual." After all, Salieri's plots against Mozart's fame ultimately failed, and yet he has been punished, by reason of the evil legend that clings to his name, with almost total obscurity for his own works. Minor instrumental works of Salieri are available on commercial recordings, but none of the operas or choral works that made his reputation. Has not the time arrived to turn from the documentation of Mozart's death to an investigation of the music of Salieri? Perhaps such a study will provide evidence that even without his adroitness in Viennese opera politics and his prestigious positions, Salieri would have afforded substantial musical competition to Mozart.

CHAPTER SIX

New Gaslight on Jack the Ripper

In China each year in rotation brings its new symbol—the year of the Hare, the year of the Dragon, etc. However, in some dark corner of the English psyche it is always the Year of the Ripper. It is forever the fall of 1888, when in the space of ten weeks Jack the Ripper hunted down his victims within the dimly lighted recesses of Whitechapel, in London's East End.

Although the English have never forgotten Jack the Ripper, he has had a remarkable revival since 1970, and there have recently been a number of sensational claims to have established his identity. We have been told that Jack was none other than the Duke of Clarence. With equal assurance, another writer asserts that he was a boyfriend of the Duke of Clarence and a cousin of Virginia Woolf. Worst of all from the point of view of the profession to which I belong is a third theory, which claims that he was a crazy lawyer. The BBC devoted a four-hour television series to the Jack the Ripper case and the principal suspects. And when I was in London at the time of the eighty-sixth anniversary of the famous crimes, the musical comedy *Jack the Ripper* had its premiere. All the favorite suspects were presented but, I am glad to say, the crazy lawyer was changed to a crazy evangelist.

Whenever newspaper articles or television programs feature the case, countless letters and telephone calls are received from Englishmen claiming descent from Jack the Ripper. Before we laugh at our English cousins, it is only fair to note that a large number of Americans claiming membership in the Mayflower Society derive their descent from a passenger on that famous ship who was later hanged as one of America's first murderers.

Why is it that the Ripper case continues to hold such fascination for the English public, and that after all these years so many journalists and writers are making serious or mock-serious efforts to unravel the secret of his identity?

Certainly murder itself held no great fascination for the nineteenth-century residents of London's East End. The cries of murder or violence were such common nocturnal experiences there that one would not be inclined (as one is today) to attribute to urban indifference the unwillingness of neighbors to rush out and investigate. However, the crimes of the Ripper were given some flavor of exoticism for England and the balance of Europe by their setting. This part of London, a concentrated area of approximately one-quarter mile which lies to the east and north of the Tower of London, was inhabited by Jews and other immigrants from Central and Eastern Europe and was ordinarily the subject of only occasional excursions, at most, by West Enders who came to take a compulsive interest in the crime. The localization of the murders led to inescapable suggestions that the Ripper was either an inhabitant of the East End or was for some reason very familiar with its haunts and escape routes. Another terrifying aspect of the crimes was their concentration in time. The earliest murder attributed without dispute to Jack the Ripper occurred on August 30, 1888, and his last crime took place on November 9. It was strange, too, that far from attempting to hide his murders, the Ripper seemed (except in the last murder) to take pains to commit them in open areas where the bodies were sure to be discovered early. Furthermore, he seemed to choose times when throngs of people would be about. The first four crimes were committed on weekends, and the final murder, of Mary Kelly, on a holiday, the Lord Mayor's Day, when the East End was bound to be unusually crowded. Although fog is legendarily associated with the Ripper murders, the fact is that the nights of the crimes were clear and that on at least one occasion the Ripper escaped apprehension by a hair's-breadth, and only because of his knowledge of East End byways. Certainly the most sensational feature of the Ripper crimes was their mounting brutality, which culminated in the almost unparalleled mutilation of his last victim.

The English are very scholarly about their crimes, as they are about all things. And just as musicologists are exceedingly demanding in their acceptance or rejection of doubtful entries in the Mozart canon, so the English are reluctant to admit doubtful crimes into the canon of Jack the Ripper. It is generally accepted that there are only five murders that bear the mark of the Ripper, even though these crimes were preceded and followed by murders that have at least some resemblance to his undoubted deeds. The first victim of the Ripper was Mary Nichols, who was found in Bucks Row on August 31. Eight days later Annie Chapman was found in a backyard at Hanbury Street, with even more severe mutilation.

On September 30 the so-called double event occurred. Elizabeth Stride was found outside a workmen's club at Berners Street. Only her throat had been cut and it seemed that the Ripper had been interrupted in the course of his crime. Later that night he murdered Catherine Eddowes, whose body was discovered nearby in Mitre Square. Finally, on November 9, Mary Kelly was found in a room in Miller's Court, the victim of almost unbelievable mutilation. Hers was the only murder the Ripper had committed indoors, as if he had intended to cap his career with an uninterrupted blood orgy.

There was, of course, a link that tied the victims together. All the murdered women were what the Victorians called "unfortunates" and what we in our franker vocabulary refer to as prostitutes. The first four victims were clearly past their prime, but Mary Kelly was a young woman of considerable beauty. The brutality of the Ripper murders was of course manifestly un-English, and the London public believed that the culprit must be a foreigner.

The Ripper was not only more violent than the average Englishman; he was decidedly more energetic. One reader wrote to *The Times* that "the celerity with which the crimes were committed is inconsistent with the ordinary English phlegmatic nature." A rumor was spread that the criminal was a mysterious personage known as "Leather Apron," so named after an article of clothing he was reported to have been seen wearing. Shortly after the second murder, a Polish Jew employed as a shoemaker, John Pizer, was captured under the suspicion of being Leather Apron. Searching his premises, the police took possession of five sharp long-handled knives which were used in Pizer's trade. He was soon freed, but there followed sporadic anti-Semitic incidents in the East End. Other favorite suspects included sailors, butchers and any unlucky persons found to be carrying black oilcloth bags, which were for some reason associated with the Ripper. This formerly fashionable item soon dropped out of the marketplace.

The fears of the public were fed by the blundering of the police who were handling the criminal investigation. The comic highlight of the police effort was the employment of two bloodhounds, Barnaby and Burgho. There was a contemporary report that, after fruitless tracking of the criminal, the dogs finally gave up and escaped, and that an alert was then put out for them. I regret that this rumor is now discounted, because the discovery of the dogs and their return to the kennel, if it had really occurred, would have been the only successful capture made by the police in the Jack the Ripper case.

In view of the widespread public terror, it is not surprising
that a number of eminent personages stepped forward to
express their opinions on the identity of the Ripper and to
offer their advice to the investigation. The most eminent of
these amateurs was Queen Victoria herself. No doubt com-
paring her own idyllic married life with Jack the Ripper's
ruder attitudes toward the female sex, the queen decided
early in the game that he could not be a married man. Moreover, despite the impeccable manners of Prince Albert, the
queen also assumed that the murderer was from the Continent. She put the following questions to the Home Secretary: "Have the cattle boats and passenger boats been examined? Has an investigation been made as to the number
of single men occupying rooms to themselves? The murderer's clothes must be saturated with blood and kept somewhere. . . ." After the murder of Mary Kelly, she had the
following hints for Scotland Yard: "All these courts must be
lit, and our detectives improved."

The young George Bernard Shaw, who was then a music
critic in London, gave a characteristically political twist to
the case. He suggested that Jack the Ripper might be a rather
splashy social reformer who had set out to expose the dismal
living conditions in the East End: "Whilst we conventional
Social Democrats were wasting our time on education, agita-
tion and organization, some independent genius has taken
the matter in hand, and by simply murdering and disem-
bowelling four women, converted the proprietary press to an
inept sort of Communism."

Meantime Jack the Ripper, show-off that he was, was en-
gaging in his own correspondence. He mailed to a builder
named George Lusk, the chairman of the Whitechapel Vigi-
lance Committee, a small cardboard box containing half a
kidney, which apparently had been removed from the body
of Catherine Eddowes. It was addressed "from Hell" and was
signed: "Catch me when you can, Mr. Lusk." Other letters,
received by the police, were of more doubtful authenticity,
including the following verse: "I'm not a butcher, I'm not a

Yid, nor yet a foreign skipper, but I'm your own light-hearted friend, Yours truly, Jack the Ripper." There was also a variant of Ten Little Indians, which began "Eight little whores, with no hope of heaven, Gladstone may save one, then there'll be seven."

Where Queen Victoria and Bernard Shaw led, hundreds have followed. The gallery of suspects is now overcrowded, and I will introduce only the leading figures among them.

From the very beginning there was considerable suspicion that Jack the Ripper belonged to the medical profession. Some observers claimed that his mutilations showed a degree of anatomical skill. However, the modern forensic pathologist Francis Camps writes that "any surgeon who operated in this manner would have been struck off the Medical Register." Nevertheless, the first modern work on the Ripper case, written by Leonard Matters in 1928, identifies Jack the Ripper as a London doctor to whom Matters gave the fictitious name Stanley. Matters asserted he had learned from "the recital of an anonymous surgeon in Buenos Aires" that Jack the Ripper was a doctor whose son had died from syphilis contracted from an East End prostitute. According to Matters's informant, this prostitute was Mary Kelly and the earlier victims of the Ripper had been struck down in the course of his search for the guilty girl.

In view of the continuing struggle for women's liberation, I am glad to say that there is a counterpart to the Dr. Stanley theory, in which Jack the Ripper is a woman. The English call her Jill the Ripper, but being a nativist at heart, I prefer to call her Jackie. One variant of this notion is that Jackie was a midwife who botched an abortion and committed a series of similar murders to cover up her malpractice. The difficulty with this theory is that only the final Ripper victim, Mary Kelly, was found to be pregnant. Another version of the midwife idea is that Jackie had been sent to prison as a result of testimony by East End prostitutes and had emerged with a hostility toward the entire profession.

By far the most exotic theory is Donald McCormick's prop-
osition that Jack the Ripper was a czarist secret agent who
was hired by the Russian secret service to commit the crimes
in order to show up the inefficiency of the English police.
McCormick bases his solution on the supposed discovery of
a French manuscript left by Rasputin at his death, on the
subject of great Russian criminals. The monk's loyal daughter, Miss Rasputin, challenges this evidence by denying that
her father, however bad his reputation, committed the ultimate crime of writing French.

Students of the subsequent history of English crime have
offered us as alternative suspects a pair of poisoners, Neill
Cream and George Chapman. Some criminologists doubt
that poisoners would be inclined to use the more brutal
methods of the Ripper. But even putting such theorizing
aside, additional difficulties present themselves. It is true that
Neill Cream displayed one of the Ripper's strange characteristics, namely, compulsive letter-writing to the police. And,
indeed, he is reputed to have said just as he was about to be
hanged, "I am Jack the—" Unfortunately, however, Cream
was in prison in Joliet, Illinois, at the time of the Ripper
murders. This presents no problem for Donald Bell, the most
recent exponent of the Cream theory. Mr. Bell, impressed no
doubt by the history of some recent elections in Cook
County, surmises that Cream actually won his freedom earlier and bribed the prison authorities to falsify the records.

The second of the poisoner suspects was Severin Klosowski, known as George Chapman by the time he was convicted
and hanged for arsenic poisoning in the early years of the
twentieth century. One of the principal bases for the suspicion of Klosowski was that he arrived in London by ship
shortly before the Ripper murders. However, it has been
pointed out that if you are going to accuse someone of the
Ripper murders merely because he was a new arrival on the
scene, you could with equal persuasion accuse the millions of
Londoners who were already there.

Even the Salvation Army has not been devoid of suspects. General Booth, head of the Army, had doubts about his secretary, who, according to the general, had "dreams of blood." I have never taken this story seriously since I do not believe that the good people of the Salvation Army have homicidal impulses, but just to cover all bets I generally give a half dollar to the Army member who solicits outside of the state liquor store in my neighborhood.

The noblest suspect of them all is the Duke of Clarence, Queen Victoria's grandson and heir to the throne of England at the time of his death in 1892. This suggestion was first published in 1970 in an article in the English crime magazine *The Criminologist,* by an elderly surgeon, Thomas Stowell. Although Dr. Stowell was careful to refer to his suspect as "S," his description clearly pointed to the duke. He alluded to the suspect's nickname, "Collars and Cuffs," which referred to his extravagant mode of dress, and mentioned a photograph of "S" showing a four- to four-and-a-half-inch starched collar and two inches of shirt cuff at each wrist. Dr. Stowell reports that the aristocratic suspect took a cruise with "high-spirited boys," one of whom seduced the duke and gave him syphilis, of which he died at age twenty-eight. Stowell outlined his suspect's army career, which began at age twenty-one and ended with his resignation at twenty-four after a raid on a male brothel in Cleveland Street, off Tottenham Court Road. Not long ago *The New York Times,* stretching its idea of what is fit to print, reported the disclosure of English court records identifying the Duke of Clarence as one of the habitués of the Cleveland Street brothel. All this makes very titillating reading, but the theory crumbles against the unyielding fact that the duke was in Scotland during the murder of Catherine Eddowes and was in Sandringham when Mary Kelly was dispatched. Nevertheless, Dr. Stowell deserves credit for ingenuity in reversing a Rousseauan concept and producing a new tradition of the "savage noble."

Dr. Stowell did not survive to stand cross-examination. He died shortly after the publication of the notorious article, and his son burned all his father's records.

Dr. Stowell claimed to have based his revelations on the private papers of the late Sir William Gull, physician to Guy's Hospital and physician in ordinary to the royal family. The Duke of Clarence's recent biographer, Michael Harrison, does not dispute Dr. Stowell's claim to have had access to such papers, but believes that he misunderstood the reference to the mysterious S. Harrison argues that S was not the Duke of Clarence but a boyfriend of the Duke of Clarence, a cousin of Virginia Woolf named James Stephen. From now on if anyone asks me, "Who's afraid of Virginia Woolf?" my answer will be: "Nobody, but I'm scared to death of her cousin."

We arrive next at one of the most fashionable of the current theories, advanced by the journalist Daniel Farson, which states that Jack the Ripper was a crazy lawyer named Montague Druitt, who drowned himself in the Thames at the end of 1888. As early as 1899, a history of crime written by Major Arthur Griffiths stated that one of Scotland Yard's three principal suspects was a young doctor who had drowned himself shortly after the murder of Mary Kelly. Farson presented a television program on Jack the Ripper in 1959. Subsequently he received a letter from a Mr. Knowles in Australia concerning a document Knowles had seen there called "The East End Murderer—I Knew Him," by Lionel Druitt. Later Farson was given access to the notes of Sir Melville Macnaghten, who joined Scotland Yard as assistant chief constable in 1889 and became head of the C.I.D. in 1903. Macnaghten indicated that one of the principal suspects was M. J. Druitt, a doctor aged about forty-one years and of fairly good family, whose body was found floating in the Thames on December 3, 1888. Farson's research revealed that Druitt was in fact a barrister who was related to two London physicians of the same name. Unfortunately, the dossier containing Farson's letter from Mr. Knowles and his other researches on Druitt vanished from Television House in London. By now, I am sure, you are beginning to gather that anonymous conversations and missing records are hallmarks of Ripper research. Farson claims to have substantiated some of the details of Knowles's letter by on-the-spot inquiries in Australia, but the document "The East End Murderer—I Knew Him" has never turned up. In the meantime, neither I nor the American Bar Association will concede that Jack the Ripper was a lawyer.

The contemporary prejudices against Jews and butchers appear to survive in the theory of Robin Odell that Jack the Ripper was an Orthodox Jewish butcher. To this intriguing suspect I have given the name Jake the Ripper, since his adoption of the public nickname Jack was presumably an assimilationist gesture. Odell explains that an Orthodox butcher would have had community standing similar to a rabbi's; and that it was on the basis of this high dignity that he won the friendship of his unwitting victims. I have never understood that Orthodox rabbis were on such easy social terms with English and Irish girls, and perhaps many of us have chosen the wrong field.

Recently, Richard Whittington-Egan has proposed still another Ripper suspect, Captain Donstan, a practitioner of black magic. One of the strongest pieces of evidence against the captain is that he had blood stained bow ties. The Donstan theory is the third within the past few years to have been pronounced by Colin Wilson to be the definitive solution of the case.

I have reported so many theories that perhaps I may be permitted to add one of my own. It appears to me that a very likely suspect emerges from an eyewitness description of the Ripper at one of the inquests cited by Dr. Stowell in his article in *The Criminologist.* In that testimony a man who was in the company of one of the victims shortly before the murder is described as being about thirty years of age, five feet nine inches tall, and wearing a deerstalker cap, with a peak in front and behind. It is my own theory that Jack the Ripper may have been none other than the distinguished Victorian detective Sherlock Holmes.

The Jack the Ripper case has left an interesting legacy in literature and music. The first important literary reflection was in the Lulu plays of Frank Wedekind. Wedekind was in London shortly after the murders, when the crimes were still on everybody's lips. In the conclusion of the second Lulu play, Lulu, a female earth spirit, is murdered by her nemesis and male counterpart, Jack the Ripper. The English at the time of the murders and for that matter ever since seem to be uncomfortable with the idea of a sexual murder. It is perhaps for that reason that they have produced so many theories trying to attribute more rational motives to Jack, such as revenge for infection. About as far as they are usually willing to go in the direction of acknowledging abnormality is to accuse a butcher of an occupational aberration. However, the idea of lust murder, or *Lustmord*, is unfortunately only too comprehensible for the Germans, and Wedekind has perhaps given us the most accurate portrayal of the Ripper, as a man of sexual violence heightened by repression.

A more demure Jack the Ripper appears in an Edwardian novel by Marie Belloc Lowndes, *The Lodger*. Her murderer is named Mr. Sleuth. Perhaps in giving him this name she shared my suspicion of Sherlock Holmes. In any event, Mr. Sleuth is a single gentleman lodger such as Queen Victoria in her own armchair work had in mind. The Victorian fear and suspicion of single gentleman lodgers was a very real one and was satirized by Dickens in *Our Mutual Friend* (1864). The fear was a response to the growing rootlessness of urban society. The murderous Lodger in the Belloc Lowndes novel is a Bible-reading vegetarian teetotaler who pins to his victims' clothing the signature "The Avenger." The sins he is avenging have been upgraded or downgraded (depending on your point of view) from prostitution to alcoholism.

The Lodger has been made into a series of motion pictures, including the 1926 silent-film classic by Alfred Hitchcock. This film begins with a close-up of a screaming blond victim; all the murder victims are blond. In an early scene in a beauty parlor, one of the women advises total abstention from peroxide until the maniac is caught. This Hitchcockian twist suggests another possible suspect—a brunette persuaded to the point of dementia that blondes *do* have more fun. Eventually it turns out that Hitchcock's Lodger has been wrongly suspected. The director had no choice, since his actor Ivor Novello was a matinee idol who would not have been accepted as a murderer.

In 1960 *The Lodger* was set as a first-rate opera by the English composer Phyllis Tate. In her version the Lodger is firmly identified as Jack the Ripper.

The French have taken a lighter approach to the case. In 1937 director Marcel Carné spoofed the Ripper crimes in a film entitled *Drôle de Drame*. This film made fun of the incompetence of Scotland Yard and also turned the butcher theory on its head. Jean Louis Barrault played a Limehouse killer who specialized in the slaughter of butchers. Like the Lodger, Barrault's killer was a vegetarian. However, he avenged sins not against abstention but against his animal friends.

One of the most recent satires of Jack the Ripper was the musical comedy of that name, mentioned earlier. All the principal suspects were introduced, but the main character was Montague Druitt, who, as I said, was changed from a lawyer to an evangelist, much to my approval. The actor portraying Druitt bore a strong resemblance to Peter Sellers, so I suppose we must add Mr. Sellers to our list of suspects. Mary Kelly was played by a beautiful actress, and you will be glad to know that her life was spared at the end.

One of the finest short stories based on the Ripper murders is Thomas Burke's "The Hands of Mr. Ottermole." This fiction produces yet another professional suspect, namely, a policeman whose beat is the East End, where the murders were committed, a policeman whom Burke gives the double animal name Ottermole. Burke's solution explains both why the Ripper was so successful in escaping attention and why the local police never seemed quite to arrive on time. The story also serves as a useful warning to journalists intent on discovering the truth of the crimes, for it ends with a reporter triumphantly confronting Sergeant Ottermole as the Ripper, only to be murdered for his candor. The reporter springs on the sergeant the question: "Now, as man to man, tell me, Sergeant Ottermole, just *why* did you kill all those inoffensive people?" I will let Burke's conclusion serve as mine:

The Sergeant stopped, and the journalist stopped. There was just enough light from the sky, which held the reflected light of the continent of London, to give him a sight of the sergeant's face, and the sergeant's face was turned to him with a wide smile of such urbanity and charm that the journalist's eyes were frozen as they met it. The smile stayed for some seconds. Then said the sergeant: "Well, to tell you the truth, Mr. Newspaper Man, I don't know. I really don't know. In fact, I've been worried about it myself. But I've got an idea—just like you. Everybody knows that we can't control the workings of our minds. Don't they? Ideas come into our minds without asking. But everybody's supposed to be able to control his body. Why? Eh? We get our minds from lord-knows-where —from people who were dead hundreds of years before we were born. Mayn't we get our bodies in the same way? Our faces—our legs—our heads—they aren't completely ours. We don't make 'em. They come to us. And couldn't ideas come into our bodies like ideas come into our minds? Eh? Can't ideas live in nerve and muscle as well as in brain? Couldn't it be that parts of our bodies aren't really us, and couldn't ideas come into those parts all of a sudden, like ideas come into—into"—he shot his arms out, showing the great white-gloved hands and hairy wrists; shot them out so swiftly to the journalist's throat that his eyes never saw them—"into *my hands!*"

CHAPTER SEVEN

M. Tullius Cicero for the Defense

The emphasis history has placed on Marcus Tullius Cicero's roles as politician and orator has somewhat obscured the fact that he was one of the most celebrated trial lawyers of his time. His experience in the Roman courts was long and varied. However, probably none of his cases was more unusual than that of Aulus Cluentius Habitus, tried in Rome in 66 B.C.

Cicero, who was then forty years old, held the post of praetor, a high judicial post second in rank only to the office of consul, to which he was aspiring. As praetor, Cicero presided over a court having jurisdiction in cases of extortion by Roman officials, but he was free to continue practicing as a trial lawyer in the other courts.

The case that Aulus Cluentius Habitus brought Cicero was one of the most sensational in Roman criminal annals. Cluentius was charged under two sections of a criminal statute adopted in 81 B.C., during the rule of the senatorial dictator Sulla. Under the first count of the complaint, Cluentius was charged with having caused the death of his stepfather, Oppianicus, by having an agent give him poison concealed in a piece of bread. It appeared at the trial that Cluentius was also accused of two other poisonings, but it is not clear whether these additional accusations were part of the formal charge or were just to show that he had acquired considerable skill in the poisoning line.

The second count alleged that prior to causing the death of Oppianicus, Cluentius had brought about his ruin and exile by falsely charging that his stepfather had attempted to poison him and by securing a conviction through bribing the jury that heard the case.

Cluentius's legal predicament can be understood only in the light of Roman criminal law as it had developed by the time of his case. Curiously enough, that stormy period from the struggles of the agrarian and social reformers, the Gracchi, beginning in 133 B.C., through the death of the dictator Sulla, in 78 B.C., was also marked by great development in Roman criminal law and in the criminal courts. The laws and court system which evolved were in many ways unlike our own. In the field of substantive law, there was no effort made during this period to prepare a unified criminal code. Instead a series of individual criminal statutes were passed dealing with specific crimes that had come to be recognized as posing special dangers to Roman society. Surely, many of these crimes had been punishable since ancient times under more loosely defined categories of criminal conduct, but the new statutes, many of which bear the name Cornelian Laws in reference to their sponsor, Cornelius Sulla, defined a great variety of crimes with considerable particularity. Under Sulla's legislative system, the crimes against which specific statutes were directed included, in addition to murder: treason, organized conspiracies to influence elections and election frauds, embezzlement of state funds, violence, rioting and intimidation, forgery and fraud, extortion, and illegal assumption of citizenship.

Some of these statutes bring into interesting juxtaposition crimes that more mature legal systems might consider quite unrelated. Thus the statute under which Cluentius was to be tried was entitled the Cornelian Law of Murderers and Poisoners. Separate sections, as reconstructed in the light of the writings of Cicero and the imperial jurists, dealt with (1) murder by the use of weapons or carrying weapons for the purpose of murder or robbery and (2) the preparation, sale, purchase, possession or administration of poison for the purpose of murder. The specification of different methods of murder in a single statute is familiar to us from our own legal system, but of greater interest is the fact that the Cornelian murder statute included another clause (founding the basis for the second count of the accusation against Cluentius) directed against conspiring or giving false testimony for the purpose of causing the condemnation of a defendant in a criminal jury trial. Although the scope of the latter section was subject to certain significant limitations, which had an important bearing on Cicero's defense of Cluentius, it is extremely moving and instructive for us to recognize that to the Romans of the late republic, the destruction of a man's life or career through abuse of the courts was a judicial murder, a murder to be condemned in the same terms and tried with the same procedures as a poisoning or a lethal thrust of the dagger.

Another respect in which the criminal law system of the late Roman republic differed from ours was that instead of setting up courts of general jurisdiction to hear all criminal offenses, the Romans entrusted each category of crimes to a specially constituted court, usually created by the same statute that defined the offense.

Thus Cluentius was to be tried in Rome before the Roman murder court to which cases under the Cornelian Law of Murders and Poisoners were consigned. In contrast to the Anglo-American system, the Roman system generally left the prosecution of criminal charges in private hands. A criminal prosecution was not instituted by a public functionary, but by a private citizen represented by a lawyer of his own choice. There was no requirement even that the prosecutor have a personal stake in the case. Any Roman citizen had standing to institute a prosecution, regardless of his motives.

In the case of Cluentius, the prosecution had been instituted by Cluentius's stepbrother, Oppianicus, Jr. However, if we are to accept Cicero's version of the affair, this formal complainant may have been a cat's-paw for the defendant's mother, Sassia, who had her own reasons for seeking his destruction.

The young Oppianicus had engaged as prosecuting attorney Titus Accius of the town of Pisaurum. During his speeches at the trial, Cicero was to have some harsh words for his opponent and his tactics. However, Cicero later wrote what may be a more objective assessment of his adversary's talents. He described Accius as "a painstaking speaker and tolerably eloquent; he was moreover trained in . . . precepts . . . which though they do not supply the richer embellishments of oratory, yet furnish outlines of argument ready made and applicable to every type of case—spears, as it were, ready fitted with straps for the skirmisher to throw."

The case against Cluentius was to be tried before a jury, as were all the crimes referred to earlier. The number of jury members varied from court to court; the number provided under the murder statute was thirty-two. All the republican juries were in theory blue-ribbon juries, since the jury rolls were supposed to be made up of persons of great experience and high repute. The Romans, however, did not pick these persons from the public at large. They imposed certain class qualifications for jury service, which proved to be a crucial point in the Cluentius defense.

The most vital point of all, however, was the penalty to be imposed if Cluentius was found guilty. The statute itself states clearly that murder is a capital offense. However, we have no record in all the writings of Cicero that during his lifetime a Roman citizen was actually executed after completion of regular proceedings in a criminal jury court. In the late republic, as the result of time-honored custom apparently aided by subsequent statutory limitation of the power of the magistrates, a Roman citizen even after conviction for a capital offense was given a reasonable period of time to escape execution by leaving Rome and taking up citizenship abroad. It might strike us as close to practical truth to conclude, then, that the punishment provided for Roman citizens convicted of capital offenses was exile. But Cicero prided himself on the fact that no Roman statute prescribed loss of citizenship as a penalty. Valuing Roman citizenship as highly as they did, the Romans preferred to see their system of capital punishment as giving the convicted man a choice between accepting death or departure from Rome and a self-willed change of citizenship.

We come now to the case that Cluentius asked Cicero to defend. The young man, a resident of Larinum in Apulia, had a rather extraordinary family background. His alleged victim, the older Oppianicus, was, even if we are to discount much of Cicero's version of the case, one of the blackest recorded examples of the mass murderer for gain, rating a place in this unlovely field of activity with William Palmer of England and Landru of France. He was reputed to have murdered at least a dozen persons, generally for pecuniary motives. His favorite weapon was poison, but he also used political proscription or hired assassins to suit the occasion. His victims included a brother-in-law, his first wife, his brother's pregnant wife and his brother. He was claimed to have murdered his mother-in-law and a wealthy young man after forging their wills in his own favor. He was said to have bribed the wife of his brother-in-law to procure an abortion in order that her husband's estate might go to Oppianicus's own son.

The most shocking rumor about the deceased Oppianicus was that he had murdered two of his three sons at the request of Cluentius's mother, Sassia, who demanded the murders as the price of her consent to Oppianicus's suit for marriage. The murders were said to have been duly performed. Sassia and Oppianicus married and accordingly formed a criminal duo that, despite their more primitive weaponry, would have been more than a match for Bonnie and Clyde.

Sassia, as Cicero was later to portray her, was an accomplished villainess in her own right. She fell in love with her daughter's husband and later married him after forcing her daughter into divorce. It was Cicero's contention that Cluentius's disapproval of his mother's conduct was the original cause of her inveterate hatred for him. Reference has already been made to the charge that Sassia required two murders as the price of her marriage to Oppianicus. Her motive was reputedly the preservation of Oppianicus's estate for her own line. The picture of this bloody wedding may be completed by adding the illuminating footnote that she had become widowed and available for the marriage to Oppianicus only because he had murdered her previous husband.

J. A. Froude saw in the story of Oppianicus and Sassia a mirror of the decay of "private virtue" in the late republic. Anthony Trollope commented that none of Cicero's other cases tells us more of "the possibilities of life among the Romans of that day."

Whatever their reasons, both Sassia and Oppianicus became the bitter enemies of Cluentius. Cluentius had been involved in a minor local political squabble with Oppianicus, but Cicero suggests that Cluentius's greatest mistake was to have remained without a will. This may have provided Oppianicus with a motive to add another relative to his long list of victims.

In any event, Cluentius claimed that Oppianicus attempted to poison him. An agent of Oppianicus delegated a servant, Scamander, to bribe the slave of Cluentius's doctor to administer poison to Cluentius. The plot was discovered through the honesty of the doctor's slave, and Scamander was taken with both the poison and the proposed bribe on his person. First Scamander and then his master, Oppianicus's agent, were tried at the instance of Cluentius under the poisoning clause of the murder statute and found guilty. Then, in 74 B.C., Cluentius brought his hated stepfather to trial. Oppianicus was convicted by a close vote. Although Cicero's accounts of the vote are not consistent, one of his orations indicates that a bare majority of the thirty-two-man jury voted for conviction. The other votes were split between votes for acquittal and abstentions, somewhat similar to the Scottish verdict "not proven."

After his conviction, Oppianicus went into voluntary exile, although, unlike most capital criminals, he seems to have been able to maintain a residence right outside the walls of the city of Rome. Shortly after his conviction, there were widespread rumors that the jury had been bribed, and in view of his conviction, much of the suspicion fell on the prosecutor, Cluentius. The alleged corruption of the jury became a political issue. Many of the persons who served on the jury were put on trial for a number of offenses, and some were barred by the censors from further public service. Some years later, probably around 70 B.C., Oppianicus died in exile. And now Cluentius stood charged under the Cornelian murder statute, first with the judicial murder of Oppianicus through the corruption of his jury and second with his physical murder through poisoning.

Cicero decided to take Cluentius's case. It is interesting to speculate about the reasons for his decision. Even though the practice of law was clearly recognized in republican Rome as a regular profession, the attorney-client relationship was very different from that of today. The activity of advocates was supposed from the earliest times to be gratuitous. The receipt of fees for legal services was prohibited by statute (Lex Cincia) as early as 204 B.C. Nevertheless, it is certain that practicing lawyers, including Cicero, received indirect compensation, often through gifts or legacies from the client or his relatives. Through his efforts at the bar Cicero himself came to own from eight to nineteen country estates, and he once told a friend that he had received what would amount today to over one million dollars in legacies. However, particularly for lawyers like Cicero, with political ambitions, more important factors in the acceptance of cases were likely to be the existence of personal relationships with the client or his friends, or political considerations. It has been suggested that some such political considerations were present in Cicero's decision to act for Cluentius.

It seems apparent from Cicero's oration that the principal charge against Cluentius was the corruption of the jury that convicted Oppianicus of the poisoning attempt. The jury had been composed, as were all juries in Sulla's time, solely of members of the senatorial class. For more than half a century jury service had been one of the primary issues on which the social factions of Rome had focused their struggles. The Gracchi are credited with legislation in the late second century B.C. that took the jury away from the senate and entrusted it to the middle-class equestrian order. During the Sullan reaction, jury service was returned to the senatorial class alone. The alleged corruption of the senatorial jury in the trial of Oppianicus was seized on by opponents of the senatorial monopoly on jury service. And in 70 B.C., under the Aurelian Law, jury service was apportioned equally among the senatorial class, the equestrian order and a related middle-class group known as the *tribuni aerarii.*

The broadening of the classes of jurors left a strange anomaly in the criminal provisions relating to judicial murder. The murder statute had been passed at a time when only members of the senatorial class were permitted to serve on juries, and the provisions banning corruption of juries were made applicable only to senators and certain other high magistrates. Even when only senators served as jurors, the limitation of the bribery statute's application to senators was not completely logical since the criminal prohibition attached not only to the receiver of the bribe but to the giver, whether or not serving on the jury, and to false witnesses. When eligibility as jurors was extended to other orders, the limitation of the bribery penalty to senators appeared still less rational, but the statute had never been amended to delete this outdated limitation. The effect of a conviction of Cluentius for judicial murder would have been to extend the application of that statute to the equestrian class and to the other nonsenatorial jurors and, indeed, to any persons, regardless of class, who gave evidence in court. Cicero, although risen to senatorial rank by virtue of the public offices he had held, was, like Cluentius, of equestrian origin and still had special sympathies with that order. These sympathies may have been a factor in his acceptance of the case.

Certainly Cicero's motives for assuming the defense must have been strong, because the defense put him in a very delicate professional and political situation. It will be recalled that prior to Cluentius's prosecution of his stepfather for the poisoning attempt, he had already been successful in securing the conviction of Scamander, the servant delegated by Oppianicus's agent to carry out the delivery of the poison. The lawyer who had conducted the unsuccessful defense of Scamander was none other than Cicero. If he now set out to prove, in accordance with Cluentius's instructions, that the alleged poisoning attempt on Cluentius was real, Cicero was sure to be faced with the argument that this position was inconsistent with his earlier position as Scamander's advocate.

Cicero was certain to encounter other charges of inconsistency if he now attempted to defend the verdict returned by the jury in Oppianicus's trial. Cicero had attacked the integrity of the old senatorial juries both in his first oration against the senatorial governor Verres, in 70 B.C., and in his oration in defense of Caecina, in 69 B.C. The Verres oration had been published and was widely known by the time of the Cluentius trial. The speech contained one particularly unfortunate detail. In an apparent reference to the Oppianicus trial, Cicero alluded in the first Verrine oration to the case of a "senator, who while he was acting as a juror, accepted money in the same case both from the defendant to divide with the other jurors and from the accuser to vote for a conviction of the accused." This allusion might now be taken by Cicero's adversary to reflect Cicero's personal view that bribery had been rampant in the earlier poisoning trial and had been practiced on both sides.

The principal source of our knowledge of Cicero's handling of Cluentius's defense is, of course, Cicero's published oration in defense of Cluentius. It is not completely clear how this speech or indeed Cicero's forensic speeches in general fit into the scheme of the actual trial procedure. The best guess is that these speeches do not represent either Cicero's opening or closing address to the jury but reflect, after polishing and editing for publication, arguments that he made throughout the course of the trial, both in his statements to the jury and in the course of presentation of evidence.

One of the principal tactics of the defense was an assault on the characters of the deceased Oppianicus and the defendant's mother, Sassia, whom Cicero portrayed as the prime motive force behind the prosecution. The catalogue of Oppianicus's murders was run through in great detail. Sassia's complicity in his murders of his sons was also presented in dark tones, together with a dramatic portrayal of the dissoluteness of her private life and the violence and recklessness of her persecution of Cluentius. One particularly effective rhetorical flourish, to which Cicero in later years made reference as an example of his exuberant youthful style, was the summary in three short, telling phrases of Sassia's theft of her own daughter's husband and her enmity to her own son in the interest of the deceased Oppianicus. Cicero described her as "the wife of her son-in-law, the stepmother of her son, the rival of her daughter."

Addressing himself to the merits of the case, Cicero gave almost all his attention to the charge of judicial murder, namely, that Cluentius had secured the conviction of Oppianicus for attempted poisoning through bribery of the jury. In view of the general belief in Rome that the jury had been bribed, Cicero did not assign himself the Herculean task of proving that no bribery had occurred. Instead he based his argument on the assumption that the jury had been bribed by only one party—either Oppianicus or Cluentius. He argued that the party who had more reason to fear an adverse result was more likely to be the briber and that that person was Oppianicus. Oppianicus, said Cicero, had great reason to fear a conviction in light of the fact that his two henchmen, including Cicero's former client, Scamander, had already been convicted, in the one case unanimously and in the other with only one dissenting vote. But if Oppianicus bribed the jury, the bribes failed to avert a conviction. Cicero explained this paradox by the treachery of the juror Staienus, who was to have divided the bribe equally among sixteen jurors (just enough to block a conviction), but decided to keep the swag for himself.

Cicero also leveled his attack on the several proceedings that had been instituted since the Oppianicus trial against various members of the jury thought to have received bribes. Cicero argued that many of the proceedings had been undertaken in the heat of political passion following the Oppianicus trial and had been premised upon charges unrelated to the alleged bribery, and that even when bribery may have been at issue, the complicity of his client, Cluentius, was not established by the verdicts. He also discounted the significance of the fact that the names of certain jurors had been stricken by the censors from the lists of those eligible for future public service, noting that actions by censors were often influenced by public opinion, subject to change and in any case not based on the careful factual inquiry required in Roman courts. He urged, too, that the senate's passage of a vaguely worded decree expressing concern about the possibility of bribery should not influence the jury against his client.

As Cicero must have expected, his opponent, Accius, did throw in his face Cicero's prior defense of Oppianicus's henchman Scamander on the poisoning attempt charge and

Cicero's speech against the corruption of the senatorial jury. Cicero attempted to justify his acceptance of Scamander's case as due to the intervention of mutual friends and his own ignorance of how bad the case was. He even tried to raise a laugh against himself by portraying how youthful and inexperienced he was at the time—how all his nervous arguments in Scamander's behalf were adroitly turned aside by his veteran courtroom adversary.

He met more directly Accius's allusion to his earlier public statement that a senatorial juror accepted bribes from both sides (an apparent reference to the Oppianicus trial). He argued that a lawyer's statements at trial must be dictated by the circumstances of the particular case before him and should not be attributed to him as expressions of his personal opinions. He said:

... I was not speaking of a fact within my personal knowledge nor did I say it in evidence: my speech was the outcome rather of the exigencies of the moment, than of my deliberate judgement. In my capacity as prosecutor I had made it my first object to work upon the feelings both of the public and of the jurors, and I was quoting, not from my own opinion, but from current rumour, every case that told against the courts, and I was therefore unable to pass over the case of which you speak, as it was then a matter of general notoriety. But it is the greatest possible mistake to suppose that the speeches we barristers have made in court contain our considered and certified opinions; all those speeches reflect the demands of some particular case or emergency, not the individual personality of the advocate. For if a case could speak for itself no one would employ a pleader.

As has been seen, Cicero's defense against the charge of judicial murder was addressed first to the merits. He contended that his client Cluentius had not been guilty of bribery. In taking this line, he stated that he was following the express instructions of his client, who, he said, was just as anxious to retain his reputation as his citizenship; Cluentius therefore insisted that Cicero waive the legal defense that the bribery statute was inapplicable. However, Cicero also engaged in an effective argument against the extension of the judicial murder clause from senatorial officials to the other classes. His political defense of his own equestrian order may have little meaning to us now, but we can continue to share with him the view, forcefully expressed, that the extension of a criminal statute to new offenses or new parties is a task for the legislature and not for a jury desiring to reach a particular result in a given case.

To the charge that Cluentius had poisoned his stepfather, Cicero, if we are to judge by his published oration, gave scant attention. In doing so, he may have been following the prosecutor's lead, since he states that the prosecutor seemed to make a "reluctant and diffident approach, for form's sake only, to the question of the charge of poisoning." Prior to dealing with the alleged poisoning of Oppianicus he dealt with two subsidiary poisoning charges. He rebutted a charge that Cluentius had poisoned a young man named Cappadox by introducing evidence of a senatorial friend of the alleged victim to the effect that Cappadox had actually died in the senator's house of natural causes. The second charge was that Cluentius, in an attempt to poison the younger Oppianicus at a wedding party, had caused another wedding guest to be poisoned when the drink was misdelivered. To disprove this charge, Cicero introduced into evidence the deposition of the father of the young man who died, to the effect that the death occurred some days later as a result of an illness. The father verified his deposition in court.

The principal defense against the ultimate charge that Cluentius had poisoned his hated stepfather was the absence of any credible supporting evidence. Apparently, the only pieces of evidence offered were unwitnessed memoranda of the alleged confession of two tortured slaves of Sassia as to their complicity in Cluentius's poisoning plot against his stepfather. However, one of the slaves reportedly had been crucified by Sassia after his tongue had been cut out, and the other slave was not produced by the prosecution. Moreover, their confessions were obtained more than three years after an earlier attempt to obtain such confessions under torture had failed. The formal reason for the new round of interrogations under torture was that one of the slaves had been found guilty of a theft of Sassia's property, and yet the memoranda of their confessions did not contain a single word about the theft. It is a blot on the record of Roman law that slaves were regularly permitted to testify only after torture. But witnesses of the first round of Sassia's tortures stopped the proceeding, observing that the object seemed to be not the extraction of the truth, but the opposite.

Cicero pointed to the clumsiness of the alleged poisoning method, the concealment of poison in bread. Why not in a drink? he asked. Why not indeed, we may add, if Cluentius had learned anything of the refined methods of his stepfather. Actually, said Cicero, Oppianicus died of a fever contracted after a fall from a horse.

The attack on the reputations of the people behind the prosecution was not a mere diversion by the defense. The Romans considered the reputations of both parties to be of more direct relevance than we do today. Cicero also introduced evidence of the good reputation of Cluentius. The evidence took the customary form of a resolution adopted by the defendant's community. But Cicero added force to the written evidence by calling attention to the large number of the defendant's well-wishers who were present in court.

It appears that Cluentius was acquitted as a result of Cicero's defense. Our principal source for this conclusion is a statement by Quintilian, the famous authority on rhetoric from the first century A.D., that Cicero later boasted that in the defense of Cluentius he had poured darkness into the eyes of the jurymen. Some commentators have interpreted this quotation to mean not that Cluentius was guilty of the alleged poisoning, but that Cicero may have clung to an earlier view that both Oppianicus and Cluentius had practiced bribery at the trial of Oppianicus's poisoning attempt.

It is interesting to note that Quintilian does not quote Cicero's boast with condemnation. To Quintilian, the purpose of the orator, whether political or forensic, was to persuade and the substitution of falsehood for the truth was an appropriate means of persuasion, so long as the orator did not deceive himself. Whatever we may think of the need for a "credibility gap" on the political scene, most of us would doubtless insist that a higher standard of conduct should prevail in the courtroom. Whether Quintilian's views on the role of factual truth in courtroom persuasion reflect Cicero's own is difficult to say. We do know that he once wrote to his trusted friend Atticus that he was considering assuming the defense of his future enemy Catiline. This letter was written only shortly after an earlier letter in which Cicero had expressed the view that Catiline would be acquitted if the jury found that the "sun does not shine at midday."

Nevertheless, whatever elements of pragmatism or indeed cynicism may be found in some of Cicero's professional or political conduct are curiously intermingled with the expression and reflection of a lofty idealism, which has proved a more permanent legacy than the practical accomplishments of his career. Regardless of our judgment as to Cluentius's relations with the notorious jury that convicted his stepfather, Cicero's defense has abiding value in its insistence on certain principles which I hope we still share, namely, (1) that matters of life, liberty and reputation should be tried in court and not by public opinion, hastily drafted senate resolutions or arbitrary actions by public officials, and (2) that criminal statutes should be interpreted narrowly and that if it is desirable to bring wider groups within their coverage, the extension should not be made retrospectively by a jury, but should be effected by a regularly enacted legislative amendment providing notice of standards applicable to future conduct.

More broadly, the Cluentius defense speaks to us today as an affirmation of the centrality of law in any civilized society. In arguing against the extension of the judicial murder statute to nonsenatorial classes without legislative action, Cicero said:

. . . Law is the bond which secures these our privileges in the commonwealth, the foundation of our liberty, the fountainhead of justice. Within the law are reposed the mind and heart, the judgement and the conviction of the state. The state without law would be like the human body without mind—unable to employ the parts which are to it as sinews, blood and limbs. The magistrates who administer the law, the jurors who interpret it—all of us in short—obey the law to the end that we may be free.

CHAPTER EIGHT

Psychological Kidnapping in Italy

The Case of Aldo Braibanti

"*Solamente una vez amé en la vida . . . Una vez, nada más, se entrega el alma.*" "Only once in my life did I fall in love," begins a Latin American song popular in this country many years ago. "Only once does one give up one's soul." The loss of a soul to one's lover may be romantic hyperbole south of the border, but in Italy it might well cost the lover a considerable term in prison. This at least is one possible reading of the strange case of Aldo Braibanti, a case that, with more justification than usual, has been stamped by journalist observers as the "trial of the century."

Aldo Braibanti was sentenced in July 1968 by the Court of Assize of Rome to nine years of imprisonment "because with physical and psychological means, in execution of the same criminal purpose, at different times he brought Pier Carlo Toscani and Giovanni Sanfratello under his own power, in such a way as to reduce them to a total state of subjection."

This charge followed verbatim the language of an obscure provision of the Italian penal code, which defines an offense called *plagio*. The English equivalent of the word *plagio* is plagiarism, and since reduction of fellow men to a state of subjection seems far removed from English notions of the limits of plagiarism, a word of explanation is necessary. There are three kinds of plagiarism under Italian law: literary plagiarism; political plagiarism, which is the impressing of a citizen of one country into the service of another; and the so-called civil *plagio* involved in the Braibanti case. In order to detect the common thread that runs through these apparently disparate crimes, recourse must be made to the Latin forebear of *plagio,* the post-Augustan word *plagium,* which denotes the crime of kidnapping or man-stealing. With assistance from this root meaning, we can see that all varieties of the crime of *plagio* involve the stealing of a human being, of his personality or of the product of his personality. Having regard for the youth of Braibanti's accusers, we can with accuracy translate the offense of which he was convicted as "psychological kidnapping."

The substance of the charge against Braibanti was that he had successively induced two young men, an eighteen-year-old apprentice electrician, Pier Carlo Toscani, and Giovanni Sanfratello, a student in his early twenties, to break their ties with families and friends and to live with him in a homosexual liaison. Although the relationships of Braibanti with the young men were separate and existed at different times, the two charges were joined, since it was alleged that his conduct with each was analogous and showed the same criminal design.

Of what did this design consist? Braibanti was claimed to have seduced the youths away from their families and their middle-class values by flattery and overrating of their limited intellectual capacities; by exalting his own genius and convincing them of their good fortune to be selected as disciples; by preaching doctrines of unlimited individual and sexual freedom and hostility to the institutionalized restraints provided by church, state and family. Once he had the youths living with him, he was said in each case to have been extremely dominant and possessive. He at times attempted to conceal their whereabouts from their families. He discouraged their contacts with outsiders and was reluctant to let them out of his sight. It was said that he invaded their intellectual privacy by requiring them to submit their dreams for his amateur psychoanalytic examination, and that he went into rages when their dreams or thoughts turned to girls or to family memories.

There was evidence that the youths were also deprived of the most basic physical privacies, including choice of attire and sleeping habits. He was said to have kept both youths for long periods in a room from which the sunlight was excluded, and in the case of Sanfratello, witnesses testified that they had seen Braibanti lock the youth in a room when he went out alone. He allegedly directed their reading and did not permit them to see newspapers or movies for fear that they would be unduly impressed by pictures of girls. Braibanti's hold over Toscani was said to have been reinforced by "magic rites," including oaths of fidelity sealed in blood and confirmed at the grave of Toscani's father.

The alleged perpetrator of this criminal design is an interesting, although apparently minor, figure on the postwar cultural and intellectual scene in Italy. The son of a doctor, Braibanti was found by the trial court to have had a difficult childhood "illuminated solely by a great love for his mother." He early showed a studious bent and interest in many fields, including the philosophy of Spinoza. During World War II Braibanti became a Marxist and entered the Resistance, fighting with the partisans. He was arrested and tortured by the Nazis. After the war he briefly took part in Communist political activity but soon withdrew, because, according to the court, "his ideas evolved towards a so-called Marcusian Marxism which is, to a certain degree, a libertarian and individualistic tendency toward anarchy."

After leaving the political scene, Braibanti turned to a great variety of cultural activities that appear to have won for him only modest recognition until the personal notoriety involved in his trial created special interest in his intellectual make-up. His activities included ceramics, the study of ants and the writing of poems, essays and dramatic works. A selection of his works was published after his trial under the title *The Prisons of State*. In these works Braibanti argues against egotism and anthropocentricity. He sees the individual united, through a rather abstract concept of love, with other individuals as embodiments of the universe, and he has a vision of man, unseated as ruler of nature, compelled to recognize his kinship with equally distant realms of microbiology and outer space. He consistently attacks the forces he sees as formalistic restraints against union with the life force and nature—the institutions of family and society, the dualism of sexual morality and the rigidity of logic and language. All the obstacles in the way of a commitment to life and a conviction of the meaningfulness of human action he grouped together as epiphanies of the fundamental anti-life principle, which he defined, in his thesis for his doctorate in philosophy, as the "grotesque."

The two young men in the case were of quite distinct personalities and backgrounds, and their relations with Braibanti followed significantly different courses. Toscani was an orphan of a factory worker and had limited education. The court concluded that he was stupefied by Braibanti's show of knowledge and that he was thrown into confusion by the conflict between Braibanti's philosophy (which he only dimly understood) and the traditional beliefs of his family. Moreover, his sexual relations with Braibanti seem to have lasted only a few months. During that period, although he was for a while working with Braibanti and spent some nights in his company, he apparently was living at home with his brother, with whom he regularly had dinner. Except on the occasion of short trips with Braibanti, he was at all times in the same city where his family lived. The court was convinced that Toscani showed no neurotic tendencies and would not permit his examination by psychiatric experts. In any event, he had sufficient strength of character to break off his relationship with Braibanti, through one of the strangest psychic agencies since Svengali's portrait taught Trilby to sing again.

As the court put it poetically, Toscani's subjection continued until "under the religious influence of the sound, unexpectedly heard, of sacred bronzes [church bells] he found for a moment the strength to run to his brother's home, in the middle of the night, and to shout to him 'Help me, I can't go on!' "

The case against Braibanti appears mainly to have been based on his relationship with the other youth, Sanfratello, and indeed the Toscani charge served the principal function of trying to show a general "design" of criminal conduct. Sanfratello was a little older than Toscani, was better educated and still a student, and his parents were alive. Signs of unhappiness and conflict with his family clearly appeared before his liaison with Braibanti, and the court's attempt to attribute them to the early stages of his acquaintance with Braibanti seems strained. Sanfratello showed a persistent tendency to take flight. In January 1960, before his affair with Braibanti, he told his family suddenly that he wanted to give up his studies, and they agreed to send him for a time to stay with a missionary priest in Paris. However, after he arrived in Paris he left the priest and went into hiding. He refused to return to his family until October, when he reappeared at home "tattered and hungry." In August 1962, after living with Braibanti in Florence for half a year, Sanfratello took flight once more. He was found by his family in Venice a month afterward, again, in the court's words, "tattered and hungry." Sanfratello later returned to Braibanti, until October 1964, when his family burst into the apartment and led him home—over Braibanti's lively objections. The evidence was that Sanfratello agreed to go with his family, while Braibanti shouted for the police, dashing to the window either to summon aid or to threaten suicide. After his return to his family, Giovanni received care in two psychiatric institutions and after his release received psychoanalytic therapy. It is reported that during his stay with Braibanti his weight dropped from 160 to 95 pounds.

Ironically, although it was the prosecution's case that San-fratello, whose relationship with Braibanti was much longer than Toscani's, had suffered more from Braibanti's dominion, Sanfratello apparently declined to be named as a formal party in the case, and his father was held entitled to become a party in his stead. Sanfratello showed concern in his testimony that he might be causing harm to his former friend.

The first legal problem with which the trial court's opinion dealt was whether the crime of civil *plagio* could be defined with sufficient concreteness to identify conduct falling under the statutory ban. Acknowledging that there was little guide provided by prior case law, the court turned to legislative history. The crime of civil *plagio* was originally provided for in the Penal Code of 1889 in language identical to that used by Article 600 of the present code for the crime of "reduction to slavery." The statutory section provided for imprisonment of "anyone who reduces another person to slavery or another analogous condition." While the code of 1889 was in effect, doubt was expressed as to whether the crime of civil *plagio* applied only to *de jure* slavery imposed by Italian citizens on others in foreign countries recognizing slavery as a legal institution, or whether it could apply also to *de facto* relations of servitude. It was to eliminate this uncertainty that in the 1930 revision of the code the original provision was split, with *de jure* situations being covered by the present Article 600, dealing with reduction to slavery, and Article 603, providing for civil *plagio*.

Despite this history, the court concluded that civil *plagio* does not merely cover cases of slavery imposed without juridical blessing under local law, but is intended to afford broad protection of the freedom of the individual personality from external interference. In the court's view the crime of *plagio* did not require physical mastery over the person, but also applied to psychological dominion, which may eventually be accompanied, but not necessarily, by material control. As a result of psychological domination by the perpetrator of *plagio,* the legal status of the victim as a free man is unaltered, but his "individual freedom," as a concrete factual entity, is suppressed. The court, stressing the fundamental, inalienable quality of human freedom in the social contract and in the constitutional setting of a republic, drew two additional threshold conclusions about the crime: (1) the victim of a crime that offends individual personality can be any person, regardless of his particular social, personal, material or psychological condition; and (2) the consent of the offended person does not justify the crime or exempt the defendant from punishment.

Not only does the consent of the victim not distinguish legal conduct from *plagio,* but, according to the court, the offense may be committed despite the absence of a specific intent to place the victim under one's power "for the purpose" of reducing him to a total state of subjection. General intent was held sufficient. That is, the prosecution need show only that the defendant consciously and willfully exercised over the victim dominion of such a nature as to reduce him to total subjection.

Although the court's consideration of the legal concept of *plagio* established as a starting point the view that the statutory section was directly concerned with the integrity of the personality, it still faced its principal task of defining the "total state of subjection" of the personality, which was the key element in consummation of the offense. It is at this point that the impression grows that the court, for all its good intentions and scholarship (the opinion runs to 180 pages), begins to lose its moorings. It announced that the statutory prohibition is justified by modern principles of dynamic psychology, which stress the key role of freedom of study, criticism and self-determination in integrating external influences into the developing personality. In the court's view, the ban against *plagio* was quite appropriately directed against suppression and distortion of the powers of judgment that are central in the development and maintenance of personality.

In considering how the purposive and critical faculties may be injured by external interference, the court ranged widely over the history of psychology and psychiatry. In addition to references to dynamic psychology, it traced the development of doctrines of suggestion from Charcot and the Nancy School. It referred also to studies relating homosexuality to psychological factors, and particularly to the findings of Ferenczi that homosexual tendencies may induce psychological states similar to obsessive or compulsive neuroses and may increase the suggestibility of the subject.

We can gather from the court's analysis of the scientific setting of *plagio* that the crime consists of the taking of action of such a nature as to impair the workings of the self-determining elements of personality and that this action may be taken through the agency of "suggestion." This is far from a satisfactory definition of criminal conduct, and a thorough search of the byways of the opinion does not add much clarity to the contour of the statutory prohibition.

The question of the psychological state of young Sanfratello, and its origin, was put to three psychiatric experts, who had examined him. Although the terms of the submission appear to be grammatically sound, one wonders what sense, if any, was conveyed to a medical mind. The question put· was:

Whether from the conduct of the accused, as it appears in the record, and also having in mind the documentary exhibits and the literary production of Braibanti to the extent it is suitable to technical evaluation of its psychological sphere, there can be derived a total state of subjection or of suggestion or of both, or any state of incapacity in Giovanni Sanfratello, stating, in the event Sanfratello is presently affected by psychological illness, the nature, origin, and course of such illness and if it can have been caused in whole or in part or accelerated in its course by the conduct of the accused or whether the same illness can have constituted a ground facilitating the action eventually directed towards placing the subject in a state of subjection or suggestion or of any other conditioning.

The experts, regardless of the difficulty they may have had in parsing, much less comprehending, this question, which, among other things, seemed to invite them to construe the undefined statutory concept of "state of subjection," were able to reply, again in statutory rather than medical language:

> From the conduct of the accused, as it appears from the record (with particular reference to the statements of Toscani) and from the description of the facts during [Sanfratello's] examination by the medical experts, it is to be concluded that a *total state of subjection* (to the causation of which suggestive mechanisms have contributed) has been created in Giovanni Sanfratello so as to bring him into the power of Aldo Braibanti. [Emphasis added.]

Asked to determine the presence of a state of either subjection or suggestion, the experts determined that, through the agency of techniques of suggestion, the *total* state of subjection required by the statute had been induced. Not only is the response in even more "hanging" terms than the question, but the experts' words indicate that they may have wandered far afield. Although they rejected the invitation to consider the "suggestive" power of Braibanti's writing, it is surprising that they found Toscani's feelings about Braibanti to have substantial impact on their psychiatric examination of Sanfratello.

The disquieting impact of this expert testimony is increased when it is observed that the court refused to permit the psychological state of the other young man, Toscani, to be passed on by the experts, on the ground that his mental health was beyond question. Not only may this omission have deprived the defense of an important line of inquiry, but the court appears to have filled the void in medical evidence by assuming the existence of a state of subjection in Toscani merely because of the similarity of some of the circumstances of the liaisons of the two youths with Braibanti. The significant differences between the two relationships, including the greater isolation of Sanfratello from his family and the greater duration of his cohabitation with Braibanti, are ignored by the court.

The arguments of the defense for psychological evidence with respect to Braibanti's personality were rejected by the court on the ground that the governing statutes do not permit expert testimony as to the personality of the accused when his sanity is not in issue. This determination, however, did not bar the court from its own speculations on Braibanti's motivational drives, including a key determination that he had a strong need to dominate which, after frustration in the political arena, led him to desire mastery of other individuals in private life. Caesar, according to the court, had become Don Giovanni.

It seems clear that "suggestion" is the main psychological mechanism the court saw at work in Braibanti's relations with the young men. The opinion appears to attempt to reinforce its weak definition of the statutory "state of subjection" by analogies to various states in which suggestion has been thought to have had a role, notably hypnosis and brainwashing. If the factual conclusions about Braibanti's treatment of the youths are to be believed, certain elements associated with hypnosis, brainwashing or other states of suggestion can be identified to a certain degree: isolation, control of physical movements, invasion of privacy, deprivation of outside stimuli and third-party relationships, unfreezing of old beliefs and indoctrination in new ideas, and the establishment of dominance over the victim. It would be proper to raise a question whether similarities to these other relationships ever could provide a safe anchor for legal definition of a crime in view of the wide divergence of scientific opinion as to the mechanisms that characterize the hypnotic state or permit coercive persuasion. But, more fundamentally, it is to be doubted that the circumstances of personal one-to-one relationships involved in the Braibanti case, how-ever stifling or degrading, bear sufficient resemblance to the controlled environment necessary for hypnosis or brainwash-ing to make comparison bear close analysis. Much of the evidence in the case suggests that witnesses as well as court had hypnosis on their minds: there is, for example, the break-ing of Braibanti's spell over Toscani by the ringing of the church bells; the witnesses' testimony that Sanfratello always walked behind Braibanti, with his eyes fixed on the ground; and Sanfratello's terrified departure from a meeting with his parents after the one hour claimed to have been allotted by Braibanti was up. However, the notion of hypnotic states lasting for months (or years, in the case of Sanfratello), and being equally effective whether the subject was in seclusion with the hypnotist or abroad in society, has a stronger affinity to the fiction of hypnosis than to the clinical or experimental literature.

Analogies to brainwashing seem no more helpful. It is fan-ciful to compare the complete physical control over the ob-ject of persuasion that exists in a prison camp setting with a relationship, however destructive, between members of an urban household. In the latter case some restraint on ex-treme conduct is imposed by prying neighbors if not by the possible intervention of friends or relatives. To compare im-prisonment with the case of Toscani, who was living at home during his "brainwashing," requires a real leap of the imagi-nation. Moreover, there is considerable support for the view that successful brainwashing may depend less on physiopsy-chological stress than on peer group pressures from other "reformed" prisoners, a social factor that would have been lacking in the Braibanti case if the evidence of the victims' isolation, which impressed the court so strongly, is accepted at face value. Moreover, it has been pointed out that if the pejorative label "brainwashing" is applied to actions outside the sphere of coercive political indoctrination of actual cap-tives, embarrassing similarities can be found with techniques of persuasion that are used in institutional or professional settings and that are socially approved. These similarities appear not only in situations involving imprisonment, such as the rehabilitation of criminals in our penal institutions, but also in settings where the actual power over the object of persuasion is social or psychological, such as in religious seminaries and psychological therapy.

Even less can be said for the court's allusion to the contemporary dangers from the "hidden persuaders" of advertising and other sectors of industrial society. Ironically, Braibanti himself attacked the "hidden persuaders" in his writings as "in their turn conditioned by their own . . . ignorance."

Having attempted to provide some basis for a decision as to what constitutes the total state of subjection required for *plagio,* the court also decided what *plagio* is not—it is not the same as love. In this conclusion, too, the court turned to psychology as its ally. It stated that "suggestive states" cannot be equated with "sentimental situations, in which the identification of the ego and the object remain distinct; love can produce identification between the object and the ego-ideal, according to Freud's conception, the super-ego, but the latter always remains separate, distinct from the ego."

Despite this flight into theory, the court can hardly have avoided the observation that much of the factual evidence of illegal domination in the Braibanti case is often associated with many instances of love and marriage—alienation from family, dominance by one partner, possessiveness, and unfreezing and changes of ideology and religious belief. On the latter point, one wonders whether the judges and jurors, if there were operagoers among them, can have forgotten Baron Scarpia's cry during the *Te Deum* at the end of the first act of *Tosca:* "Tosca, you have made me forget God!"

The court also says that lovers want to make their loved ones happy, whereas Braibanti, through his will to dominate, forced his victims to live in misery. This is quite an optimistic view of marriage, particularly in a society that until recently did not recognize divorce. It is interesting to note that a witness, who observed how submissive Sanfratello was in Braibanti's presence, added that "they were just like husband and wife."

Having dealt with the unlawful object of *plagio,* the subjection of the free personality of another, the court considered in detail the means it found Braibanti had utilized to achieve the illegal end. None of the means were unlawful in themselves.

The homosexual relations of Braibanti with the young men were not unlawful. Nor did his relations with them constitute statutory rape, since they were over the age of consent and neither of them was found to be in a mental condition that would negate their consent. Although there was evidence of Sanfratello having on occasion been locked in his room when Braibanti was going out alone, the prosecution apparently was not sufficiently sure of its ground to assert that an independent crime in the nature of false imprisonment had thereby been committed. Furthermore, no similar evidence existed in the case of Toscani. Ultimately, Braibanti's counsel was to argue on appeal that if any offense was to be charged, it should have been the charge of "private violence" under Article 610 of the Penal Code, which provides a maximum of four years imprisonment as compared with a minimum of five and a maximum of fifteen in the case of *plagio.* Private violence has been committed when one "with violence or threat, forces others to do, suffer or not to do any thing."

Of greater significance is the court's assertion of the right to consider Braibanti's inculcation of his antiestablishment and sexual views as a means of alienating the youths from their families and bringing them under his power. (We have already noted the unsuccessful attempt to have the medical experts undertake a similar analysis.) The court states rather defensively that in examining Braibanti's ideas as a means to an illegal purpose, rather than as criminal in themselves, it is escaping the injustice history has found in the trial of Socrates. Nevertheless, judicial criticism of literature is a dangerous bypath in a proceeding in which the life or liberty of author or reader is at stake. Signs of ideological and literary bias and predilection are scattered through the opinion. Braibanti's work is criticized as derivative; an early work reminds the court of Baudelaire. (The work reminds me of Moravia and Camus.) There is a surprising assault on Braibanti's early favorite philosopher, Spinoza, as a social pariah and a preacher of fatalism and resignation. The court also takes keen delight in turning against Braibanti the words of Herbert Marcuse, one of the "philosophers praised by Braibanti." It observes that Braibanti had been guilty of "repression," which Marcuse regards as society's prime ill. Despite all these comments, the court claims ideological impartiality, but its feelings are revealed when it denies that it is condemning the defendant because of his "profound amorality."

Distinctions between ends and means have been mischievous when made either by enemies of law or by its defenders. Many of those who see error in the present institutions of society would justify violence, rioting or murder in the name of what they regard as socially desirable directions of change. Conversely, the common law and its administrators appear to have served better when the legal character of an act does not change depending on whether the purpose for which it was committed is socially approved. We have been left, in the difficult cases involving advocacy of war resistance and other controversial causes, with the unhappy legacy of common-law conspiracy, which finds a crime when overt acts, legal in themselves, are committed pursuant to a prohibited design.

It is recognized that personal relationships such as that involved in the Braibanti case can be destructive. Unfortunately, the same may be said of many marriages and of many parent-child relationships. We have seen in recent years a good deal of social harm arising out of larger and less traditionally structured groups, from the street gang to the drug-oriented commune or ritualistic cult. Yet despite these dangers, the Braibanti case and the uncertainties in the processes of decision that a study of the trial court opinion reveals do nothing but reinforce the notion that the law is more at home with regulating overt acts than purposes or states of mind. It seems possible that Braibanti might not have been convicted if he had been tried under more traditional statutes dealing with overt acts, such as the provision for "private violence." Perhaps trial under these more traditional provisions, even at the high risk of acquittal, would have been better administration of justice. The satisfaction the victims or their families may have derived from the court's finding Braibanti guilty of *plagio* does not, to my mind, justify the jurisprudential harm done by the court in breathing life into this vague criminal ban.

On July 14, 1968, the trial court, composed of six jurors (four men and two women) and two judges (Judge Dr. Giuseppe Volpari and Presiding Judge Dr. Orlando Falco), found Braibanti guilty on both counts of *plagio* and sentenced him to a term of nine years imprisonment, of which two years were condoned. In determining to set the base penalty at twelve years (prior to various reductions), the court noted that it

could not help but consider the gravity of the crime flowing from the very nature of [the defendant's] conduct consisting of a plan coldly prearranged to result in the annulment of the freedom of will of others, a plan pursued with such suggestive means as would not be noticed by the victims and then working with craft and masking with friendship and affection calculated and hidden hostile conduct.

The court also took into consideration "the gravity of the harm done the victims, who were constrained to live for a long time in an intolerable state of abjection, with undoubted consequences for their health and personalities." Among the grounds for reduction of the sentence were "the meritorious patriotic actions of the accused in the period preceding his criminal conduct," for which it was proposed that four years be subtracted from the initial twelve-year term.

On November 28, 1969, the Appeal Court of Assize of Rome affirmed the conviction of Braibanti, but reduced his sentence to four years. In consideration of the preventive imprisonment suffered by Braibanti prior to his trial, the court ordered Braibanti freed on December 12, 1969.

The appeal court rejected the contention of Braibanti's lawyer that the crime of *plagio* was too vague for application. They heard as well his argument that the trial court had wrongly identified homosexuality with the politics of the left. Braibanti's lawyer argued that, on the contrary, "the Don Giovannis do not belong to the world of labor but live in the huge palaces of Catherine the Great!"

Assuming that these arguments may have missed the mark, why then the reduction of the base penalty? It appears from one newspaper account that in the end Braibanti, like the young Toscani, was saved by the bell. The appeal court agreed that Braibanti had committed *plagio* in the case of Sanfratello, but impressed by Toscani's ability to free himself from Braibanti's clutches when the carillon pealed out, concluded that in his case the total state of subjection had not been consummated and Braibanti was guilty only of attempted *plagio*.

Afterword

In 1971, Braibanti's conviction was affirmed by the Italian Supreme Court (the Supreme Court of Cassation). Recently I was informed by Italian friends that another defendant has been convicted of *plagio*, this time in the Naples area.

CHAPTER NINE

Henri de Latouche and the Murder Memoirs of Clarisse Manson

"... l'absurde vous sauve de l'horrible."

Henri de Latouche, *La Reine d'Espagne,* Act IV, Scene 1

Truman Capote clearly had no eye to literary history when he claimed to have created in his crime study, *In Cold Blood,* a new genre, the "nonfiction novel." The genre may be defined as a combination of reportage of a current event (such as a criminal case) with an imaginative commentary in which the author attempts to apply fictional talent and method to the reconstruction of the motivation or interior dialogue of the persons involved in the factual drama. Far from being a modern invention, the nonfiction novel, as a device for crime narrative, dates back at least to the early nineteenth century. One of its first notable examples in France was *The Memoirs of Madame Manson,* published in 1818 (all quotations are taken from the rare English edition, London, 1818). The *Memoirs,* which purport to have been "edited" from the original draft of Clarisse Manson, the enigmatic principal witness in the Fualdès murder trials, in fact were for the most part the original work of the versatile man of letters Henri de Latouche, who was later to find an important place in French literary and journalistic history as first editor of the poetry of André Chénier, as editor in chief of *Le Figaro,* and as mentor and sponsor of Balzac and George Sand.

Controversy had always surrounded Latouche, both in

his personal life and in his professional career. He was born in 1785 at La Châtre in the Berry region. He was of an aristocratic family, and an uncle had been named a peer of France. If Laurence Sterne is correct that many a child has been Nicodemused into nothingness, then Latouche was doomed at birth to the stylistic excesses of which his critics complained by the incredible name bestowed on him: Hyacinthe-Joseph-Alexandre Thabaud de Latouche. Married at twenty-two, he became, in the words of one commentator, "quite rapidly unfaithful." Gossip claimed that he was the father of a child born in 1810 to Marceline Desbordes, who was then a young actress and was to become, with the encouragement of Latouche, a writer of elegiac poetry.

The professional career of Latouche prior to his appearance on the scene of the Fualdès case had been varied. He had held a sinecure with the tax authorities traditionally reserved for literary men and had written some unimportant pieces for the theater. He later joined the editorial staff of the *Constitutionnel* and was personally responsible for having that periodical suppressed in 1817. Having been given the assignment of writing reviews of the art shows at the Salon, he defied the censor's blue pencil by retaining in one of his reviews a seditious allusion to the tricolor and the King of Rome. When the Fualdès case arose, he was offered the assignment of writing reports of the trial for the *Gazette de France*. His willingness to accept the assignment is attributed by some to his desire to make his name and line his pockets out of a case that seemed destined to prove a great sensation with the public. However, he is also credited with having had a strong penchant for the bizarre. In 1821, shortly after the Fualdès case, he again was to make disaster his subject, when he wrote the supposed memoirs of two victims of the plague at Barcelona. A more favorable explanation of Latouche's attraction to the Fualdès case and other spectacular events on the European scene could rest on his unremitting attachment to the profession of journalism. This profession was new enough in the early nineteenth century to account for much of the charge of sensationalism that still clings to Latouche's name. In fact, Frédéric Ségu, Latouche's principal biographer, writes that Latouche had the temperament of a reporter and was "on the lookout for news."

Certainly Latouche was correct in sensing the degree of interest the public would take in the details of the Fualdès case and in its personages. The case preoccupied public interest not only in all France but beyond its borders. Armand Fouquier writes that in Paris the Fualdès murder provided welcome relief from the fevers of renewed political activity in the capital. Therefore, despite the political significance many tried to read into the murder of Fualdès, the case served primarily as an antidote to postwar politics, much as the trial of the mass murderer Landru in 1921 at Versailles provided distraction from the aftermath of World War I.

The Fualdès murder came to light on March 20, 1817, when a woman walking by the banks of the Aveyron River outside the town of Rodez in southern France saw a body floating in the water near a mill. When the corpse was retrieved, the victim, whose throat had been cut, was identified as a well-known citizen of Rodez, the recently retired magistrate Joseph-Bernardin Fualdès. During the Revolution Fualdès had served as a juryman of the Revolutionary Tribunal and was on the jury that condemned Charlotte Corday. However, Fualdès was not a radical and had briefly served as royal *procureur* under the Restoration. Nevertheless, many persisted in seeing the death of Fualdès as the retributive work of the White Terror, which was still active in other parts of France.

The murder of Fualdès, though its solution remains in controversy to this day, probably had a more prosaic motivation. The police inquiry disclosed that on the evening before the discovery of his body, Fualdès had left his house for an appointment, carrying with him a bulky package. There was speculation that he was meeting to arrange for the negotia- tion of a considerable amount of securities which he had received as proceeds of real estate he had sold to provide for his retirement. However, Fualdès's trail led to a strange place for the transaction of such business. Investigators de- termined that he was murdered in the kitchen of the town's only brothel and house of assignation, operated by a couple named Bancal. Witnesses indicated that a crowd of murder- ers and accomplices took part in the crime and later formed a macabre cortege which brought the body to the river. M. Bancal was arrested and a number of other arrests followed. Among the principal suspects taken into custody were Ber- nard Charles Bastide-Gramont, Fualdès's godson, and Joseph Jausion, Bastide's brother-in-law, who acted as Fualdès's agent and securities broker. Despite the White Terror ru- mors, the police theorized that the magistrate was murdered either to obtain valuable securities or to cover up malad- ministration of his financial affairs.

Bancal, while in prison, made a "confession," which added a new element of mystery to the case and prepared the way for the dramatic appearance of Clarisse Manson as star wit- ness. He told police that before the murder a veiled woman had entered the kitchen and Bancal had hidden her in a closet. According to Bancal, he forgot about her presence and was astonished when Bastide found her there just after the crime had been committed. Only the intervention of Jausion prevented Bastide from murdering her, and instead Bastide compelled her to give a terrible oath of silence.

Bancal died in prison the day after his confession. The most pressing business now before the police, as well as before the gossips of Rodez, was to identify the mysterious veiled woman who had the double misfortune to be caught by many unwanted observers in the act of paying a visit to a house of ill repute, and to have become the unwilling witness of a murder on those usually convivial premises. The names of many young women were mentioned, but they soon yielded to the intriguing figure of Clarisse Manson. A young officer named Clémandot, who was aide-de-camp to General Vautré, told the prefect, Count d'Estourmel, after being pressed to do so by friends to whom he had already told the same story, that an acquaintance of his, Clarisse Manson, had confided in him that she had been at the Bancal house on the evening of March 19.

Clarisse Enjalran Manson, the daughter of a judge at Rodez, appears to have had a deep-seated taste for the romantic. In her early dreams she saw herself as a princess, or as the wife of a robber chief. Her dreams had a bitter clash with reality when, at the instance of her parents, she married an uncultured army officer, Marc-Antoine Manson. Just as contemporary accounts did not rate her a Cleopatra, so her husband was in her eyes a Mark Antony in name only. She had the poor taste to tell him that her ideal man was a certain cavalry lieutenant to whom she had given the intimate nickname Klein-King, and who in her eyes had all the mercurial and fantastic qualities her husband lacked. Manson went away to fight in Spain, and she made up her mind not to have him back again. However, when he returned, he decided that even without an exotic name like Klein-King, he could play the romantic as well as the next man. He supposedly serenaded his wife under her window. When she let down her ladder in a Pavlovian response to romantic music, she may have been shocked to see that it was her husband who was entering her room. In any event, she went along with the game for a while by granting him access to her bedroom on the condition of strict repetition of the music and ladder ritual. Finally Clarisse became bored with this routine and separated from Manson, to live alone in Rodez. Gossips were certain that she was not suffering deprivation of male society.

Clarisse had a romantic view of herself, as well as of life. To borrow words applied to a Joyce Cary heroine, Clarisse saw in the mirror "herself surprised." She liked to think herself capable of unexpected actions and to view her actions as separate from their consequences. In the introduction to her memoirs she is quoted as having written in one of her letters:

I am astonished at myself: I am inexplicable; so says my mother. I do nothing like other people. . . . I rarely calculate on the effects that will result from an action that my heart prompts me to perform, and I seldom have cause to regret it. I always act without premeditation.

From the moment of her entry into the Fualdès case, Clarisse Manson began to produce a remarkable number of different versions of her story. In reading her depositions and testimony, one has the impression of experiencing a French *Rashomon,* but with all the versions of the crime being given by a single witness. In order that her inventiveness and inconsistency can be appreciated, the various versions she produced prior to the trials will be consecutively numbered and summarized as we proceed. But no notion of how truly maddening she was to the police and judicial authorities, not to mention her family, can be accurate without understanding that she interspersed, in the intervals between her statements, depositions and testimony, emotional interviews and communications protesting her innocence and weakness, asking for protection or forgiveness, hinting at the guilt of others, and giving the impression that she was under constant threat and pressure from relatives and friends of the principal defendants to lie, to retract, to remain silent.

The first story that Clarisse Manson told the authorities on being summoned for questioning had at least the virtue of a truly Doric simplicity. Her Version One may be summarized briefly:

I deny everything which M. Clémandot has said. I hardly know him.

Version One was as short-lived as it was brief. The day after Clarisse made her first statement, the prefect received a letter from her, agreeing to a meeting with Clémandot, which the young officer had requested. Upon being confronted with Clarisse, Clémandot repeated his statements. Clarisse, in response, produced Version Two of her story, which still does not bear the marks of the genius she was later to show. Version Two may be summarized as follows:

Everything which M. Clémandot has reported about my conversation with him is correct, except that our conversation took place during the evening of July 20 and not during the night. However, I told him the story in jest. Actually, I have never been at the Bancals' house.

Version Two did not convince the prefect, nor did it satisfy Clarisse's father. Accompanied by two other persons, they took Clarisse Manson to see the scene of the crime, where she grew pale, trembled, wrung her hands and fell down in a faint. When she revived, she was taken into the Bancal kitchen and seemed to recognize the closet.

When she was returned to the prefect's office, she was ready to talk, and promptly produced a deposition containing Version Three of her story. The substance of this statement was the following:

At nightfall, on March 19, 1817, I was walking in the Rue des Hebdomadiers. In order to avoid several people whom I heard coming, I entered into an open doorway, which I later have learned to be that of the Bancal house. When I crossed the passageway, I was seized by a man who was coming either from the outside or inside the house. My confusion in the darkness didn't permit me to see. I was quickly put in a closet. A voice told me to be quiet; the door was closed and I stayed in the closet as if in a faint. I don't know how much time went by, but I heard people from time to time talking and walking around. I tried to open a door or a window and bumped my head. Then a man came into the closet, took me rudely by the arm, and made me cross a room where I could only see a weak light. Then we went out into the street. The man quickly led me to the Place de Cité. He assured himself

*that I did not recognize him and did not know where I was
coming from and had not heard anything. He said: "If you
talk, you will perish." He let me go but after I had taken
refuge under the stairs of the convent of the Annonciade he
caught up with me again. I repeated that I did not recognize
him. He said that he was not one of the murderers and that
he had let me go out of pity since I was a woman. He asked
me what I had been going to do at the Bancal house. I told
him that I had seen someone enter whom I thought I had
recognized and that I wanted to make sure.*

To the statements in her deposition Clarisse added the
information that during her visit at the Bancal house she was
disguised as a man.

The first trial of the accused murderers of Fualdès began
in May 1817. Things had been going slowly, when Madame
Manson was called to the stand at the session of August 22.
We are told that she was dressed simply, and that a veil of
tulle half covered her face. When Clarisse passed in front of
the bench on which the defendants sat, Jausion made her a
deferential bow. This gesture may have cost him his life.

The presiding judge first asked Bancal's widow if she knew
Madame Manson. Clarisse showed from the very beginning
that she would not take a passive role in the trial. She turned
sharply in front of la Bancal, lifted her veil and said firmly,
"Do you know me?" La Bancal said that she did not. Bastide
and Jausion were asked the same question by the judge.
Jausion said that he only knew her through having seen her
two or three times at his house, about four or five months
before, paying a visit to his sister-in-law Madame Pons. Clarisse took great offense at this response and cried out, "You
don't know me! Then how did you have the audacity to salute
me in open court?" After the commotion which this outburst
caused died down, Bastide responded that he did not know
Madame Manson except that he had met her once on the
highway.

The presiding judge then, in extremely affectionate terms, pleaded with Clarisse to tell what she knew about the murder of Fualdès. Clarisse's response was an effective curtain-raiser. She gave the defendants a dramatic look and then fainted into the arms of the nearest spectator, who happened to be Field Marshal Despérières. When revived with smelling salts and vinegar, she cried, "Take those murderers out of my sight!" and shook her hands about as if she were defending herself against something frightening.

The testimony that followed this drama was a distinct anticlimax, much like the fatal last act the self-indulgent playwright should have cut. She said, "I have never been at the Bancals'." After a pause, however, she won her public back by adding, "I believe that Jausion and Bastide were there."

Asked to explain this apparent contradiction, she said she based her belief on anonymous letters sent her and attempted intercessions which she ascribed to the camp of the defendants. Pressed further by the court, she said she based her belief on "conjecture." Turning to Jausion, she added a further incriminating allusion based on the public's knowledge that he had once been suspected of attempted infanticide: "When one kills one's children, one can kill one's friends, one can kill anybody."

Despite her intention to cling to the position that she knew nothing, Clarisse Manson was far from finished with her performance on the stand. The presiding judge pleaded with her "as the daughter of a magistrate" to tell the truth. The witness's reaction was again not what was looked for. She fainted once more. When she came to, her eyes first lighted upon the sword of her loyal attendant, the field marshal. She pushed him off with one hand, pointed to his weapon with the other, crying, "You have a knife—a knife." She fainted again. The marshal was gallant enough to take off his sword, and Madame Manson responded by recovering her senses.

When the presiding judge urged Clarisse to overcome her fears, she took heart and returned again to the role of cross-examiner. She requested the judge to ask Jausion if he had not saved a woman's life at the Bancals'. Jausion persisted in his denial. After another of her fainting spells, which now appeared to be punctuating her testimony quite regularly, Clarisse recounted that a M. Blanc had told her that Jausion had saved the life of a woman who had been hiding in a closet at the Bancals'. She persisted in her position that she was not that woman.

The presiding judge, in a new effort to conquer the witness's fears, ordered the army commander to place a cordon of soldiers between the witness's chair and the defendants. The court then turned to Bastide and attempted to obtain his admission that he had been in the Bancal house at the time of the murder. Bastide, interrupting him, repeated his statement that he had never had any relationship with the Bancal house, "whatever Madame Manson says." Clarisse was as stunned by Bastide's contradiction as she had been by Jausion's greeting. She interrupted him by stamping her foot and crying out, "Confess, you wretch!"

Recalled to court on September 3, after the cases of all parties were closed, Clarisse Manson had one more dramatic scene to play. When Maître Romiguières, Bastide's lawyer, addressed her in his argument, Madame Manson interrupted him: "Ah! No, all of the guilty are not in chains!"

After the arguments were over, Madame Manson was put back on the stand and produced Version Four of her knowledge of the Fualdès murder. It may be summarized as follows:

I was not at the Bancal house. However, I have learned the details of the crime from Mademoiselle Rose Pierret. I am not saying that she was the woman who was in hiding at the Bancals', but she certainly tried to give me the impression that she was.

Rose Pierret, a girl friend of Clarisse's brother Edward, was called to testify and denied that she had ever been at the Bancals'.

It is doubtful whether this new accusation by Clarisse,

against Pierret, had any impact on the trial, but her earlier outbursts seemed clearly reflected in the verdict. La Bancal, Bastide, Jausion and two others were unanimously found guilty of premeditated murder. Most of the other defendants were found guilty of lesser crimes.

Two days after the verdict, Clarisse Manson was arrested, charged with false testimony. She soon found herself in bad company. In October, the judgment of the Rodez court was reversed on the ground that the registrar had, in the case of the testimony of nineteen witnesses, failed to insert into the court record the full witnesses' oath as required by law. Since the principal defendants now had to be retried, this time in the court at Albi, the authorities decided to try Clarisse Manson with them as an accomplice. In the meantime, she languished at the Prison of the Capuchins. It was here that Latouche, who was reporting the trial for the *Gazette de France* under the nom de plume *le Sténographe parisien,* came to see her and ultimately proposed the "editing of her memoirs." It is difficult to reconstruct the birth of the collaboration of Latouche and Clarisse Manson. If we are to believe the bad press that Latouche has received from many writers, we would have to conclude that he won her confidence through conversational glitter and craftiness. Armand Fouquier wrote of him:

A sly man, a false friend, he exercised an irresistible seduction through the caresses of his voice and of his pen. But he hastened to sacrifice the best comrade to an epigram. It was he, it is said, who invented the word *camaraderie;* but one can see how he understood the concept. Vain, thin-skinned, a poseur, bitter, quarrelsome, captious, hiding his claws under velvet, de Latouche nevertheless had charming qualities of wit, vivacity and finesse, but little depth and mediocre learning. . . .He possessed a gift which, in our days, is the greater part of success: he knew how to maneuver people, and had a nose for popular fashion.

Armand Praviel, in his fictionalized *The Murder of Monsieur Fualdès,* gives a distinctly unflattering picture of Latouche as he appeared to Clarisse in her cell:

The man who was later to be the recipient of the most touching tokens of affection was distinctly ugly and had a most clumsy limp. He was carefully, though not elegantly dressed, and through the veneer of his polite manners, an underlying vulgarity could be detected.

Praviel suggests that Clarisse, who had decked herself out for the occasion in a light blue merino dress and a red woolen shawl, and a large straw hat trimmed with black ribbons, must have been disappointed by his looks and regretted the trouble she had taken.

Nevertheless, somehow Latouche was able to win her agreement to permit him to edit and arrange for the publication of her memoirs. His techniques of persuasion are probably largely matters for speculation, but it is suggested that he did not neglect flattery. Clarisse, while in prison, had turned to poetry, and had scratched some verses on the mantelpiece of her cell. It is surmised that Latouche may have recited these verses in suitably appreciative tones. In the aftermath of the publication, it was to appear that more material means of persuasion had been employed. When the moment was right, Latouche offered to purchase from Clarisse the handful of roughly drawn pages she called "memoirs." She modestly suggested that perhaps the writing had some value and tentatively requested a few francs. Latouche countered by presenting her with a purse containing twenty-five louis. But he did not leave the financial arrangements on this basis. After his return to Paris, he asked the publisher to make an immediate payment of twelve hundred francs to Madame Manson, to be followed by an equal payment three months later. Finally, with a touch of gallantry, or perhaps a mocking reference to the mysterious disguised woman in hiding at the murder house, Latouche had his publisher send Clarisse a magnificent veil of black lace.

The form and style of the Manson *Memoirs*, which resulted from the collaboration of Madame Manson and Latouche, proclaim a close kinship to the sentimental epistolary novel of the eighteenth century. Written in the form of a letter to

Clarisse's mother, the *Memoirs* invoke and trade upon family emotion—the concern of Clarisse's mother and nostalgia for the days of her protection, the anger and dominance of Clarisse's father, the gallant support of her brother and, overriding all, Clarisse's love for her little son, Edward, and fears that he is in danger and will be taken from her. In this emotional setting of family loves and fears run three separate strands of narrative: the development of the relationship between Clarisse and Clémandot; the course of her confessions, denials and court performances; and her crowning achievement, the discovery that the veiled woman at the Bancals' was Rose Pierret.

The story of the young officer Clémandot clearly had an important role in any explanation of Clarisse's conduct, but in the *Memoirs*, the early days of the acquaintance between Clarisse and the officer take on a life of their own. The spirit of the English novelist Samuel Richardson dominates the scene. Perhaps Latouche was working the materials of Clarisse's revelations in a manner designed to meet prevailing literary taste. However, it may not be too much to suggest that the name Clarisse aroused in him, and perhaps in Madame Manson herself, memories of the heroine of Richardson's popular *Clarissa*. Armand Fouquier makes this literary play on Madame Manson's name in summarizing the public expectations of Clémandot's testimony at the first trial:

It is not only the confidant of a horrible mystery which the public wants to see in M. Clémandot, it is the Lovelace of Clarisse.

Clarisse's first meeting with Clémandot did not appear to presage future intimacy. One day, while she was standing in the millinery shop of Madame Constans, a stranger came in. He talked so familiarly to the milliner "and took so many indecent liberties" that Clarisse felt "obliged to retreat hastily, without purchasing anything." She learned next time she saw Madame Constans that the stranger was aide-de-camp to General Vautré "and a zealous royalist." Clarisse did not think that either of these distinctions excused his rude behavior.

It appears that Clarisse's passion for the theater favored M. Clémandot's advances. He met her again at a theater in Rodez where a company of comedians was performing. She blames her attendance on the spirits of evil:

. . . an evil genius, bent on my destruction, inspired me with so strong a passion for the spectacle, that I could not any longer resist the inclination of being present.

On one occasion of her attendance at the comedians' performance, Clémandot, lucky to find the tier of boxes where she sat to be thinly filled, took a vacant seat by her side and launched into a praise of "the beauty, symmetry, and elegance of manner" of another young lady. With apparently more grace than logic, he followed up this conversational line with a request to be permitted to offer Clarisse his arm and see her home. She thanked him civilly, and enjoyed being able to pronounce him outranked: She had come to the theater with a *general* and his nieces and would go back with them. However, it turned out that the general had no lantern and Clémandot took the occasion to come up behind with one, efficiently lighted. The general met this unexpected assault by lighting a wax taper and Clémandot went his way.

Clarisse's escape from Clémandot was not long-lived. The very next day, while she was in the company of her brother Edward, Clémandot, who knew him as a fellow soldier, called him by name. This family contact apparently softened Clarisse's feeling to the point of her permitting Clémandot to walk with her while her brother walked ahead with his friend, Rose Pierret. Clémandot told Clarisse that he was leaving town in two days and asked unsuccessfully to be allowed to call upon her to say goodbye. Clarisse declined and, in fact, was more concerned that he seemed to be lagging behind the pace of her brother. He blamed his slow progress on his corns, but she rather unfeelingly asked him to redouble his steps. The two couples' outing appeared to last all night, being topped off by a coach trip to Espalion for breakfast. According to Clarisse's account, it was a decidedly chaste occasion.

The climactic scenes in Clémandot's pursuit of Clarisse are pure Richardson. He finally gave up reconnoitering for direct assault. One night after supper, Clarisse heard a "gentle rap at the door" and Clémandot entered. She asked him to leave, but he answered that he was not in any particular hurry. After her arguments failed, she decided to make a prompt retreat and to leave her enemy in possession of the room. Returning in about an hour, she made a careful inspection of the room, was satisfied that he had left, and went to bed. The next day she was told by her neighbor that Clémandot had visited her again in the morning. The assault was renewed after dinner, when she heard the "creaking of boots" in the corridor leading to her room, and "two distinct raps at the door," discreetly separated by a half hour's interval. Sometime later she heard another rap, and remembering that the door had been left unlocked, rushed to turn the key, but was too late.

Clémandot entered, and by this time Clarisse saw him in full light as a man from the pages of Samuel Richardson and hardly as a Richardsonian hero. She writes, with emphasis:

. . .The man, *who is anybody but Sir Charles Grandison*, pressed violently forward.

Perhaps to the disappointment of her readers, Clarisse "conjured him so pathetically to withdraw, that at last he consented."

Clarisse might have been spared another round with her antagonist had not her love for the theater intervened again. She went to the opera, where she again caught glimpses of Clémandot, who finally left, after giving her "a fierce and menacing look." Shortly after her return home, Clémandot entered her room again, and this time was careful to lock the door.

Clarisse interrupts her account of this interesting turn of events to deliver a speech worthy of Richardson's virtuous heroine, Pamela:

From that dreadful night I date all my misfortunes! What have been the sorrows of a whole life, when put in competition with those that have overwhelmed me for the last few months! How many bitter tears have I shed! O my father, mother, brothers, my son! ties ever dear and sacred, that alone reconciled me to life! without you, without the consolations of religion, I had made an attempt upon my life!

As the narrative is taken up again, it soon becomes apparent that Clarisse was referring not to the loss of her virtue, but to her involvement in the Fualdès case. Clémandot's amatory advances were impeded by heavy imbibing at a grand supper given earlier in the evening by General Vautré for his staff. When he tried to embrace her, Clarisse easily pushed him to a corner of the room. He refused her entreaties to go, and announced his intention to stay until three o'clock in the morning, the hour fixed by the general for the departure of his troops. The remainder of his accomplishments in that room were hardly in keeping with the self-advertisements he had made during the trip to Espalion:

He yawned repeatedly, and fell asleep, or pretended to do so.

He woke up after half an hour and, according to Clarisse, it was at this point that the fateful conversation about the Fualdès case occurred. He told her that he had something very interesting to communicate to her. It was reported, he said, that a young woman had been at the Bancals' during the murder. One person had accused Mlle. Avit, the daughter of the court registrar. Clarisse interrupted him, saying that she did not believe that Mlle. Avit would have entered a house of such poor reputation. However, the registrar's daughter appears to have been merely an opening gambit, since Clémandot went on to say that some other people "pretended" that Clarisse had made an assignation at the Bancal house, and that Bancal's wife, hearing footsteps, had concealed her in a place where she could see and hear everything.

In her version of what then transpired, Clarisse maintained that her "confession" was in jest:

I looked at him with astonishment. "Come," cried he, "was it not you?" "Come, confess it was."—"Oh!" I replied, "certainly; there can be no doubt of it!"

Clémandot gratefully replied:

"Poor creature, how interesting this makes you in my eyes!"

Clarisse, in explaining this interview, claimed that she had not the smallest doubt that Clémandot was either insane or intoxicated, although his drowsiness inclined her to the latter view. He talked very loud, and met her requests to lower his voice by breaking into song. She won his silence with a cup of chocolate and at last prevailed on him to leave.

At this point in the *Memoirs* M. Clémandot leaves the foreground to remain as an opponent of Clarisse in her encounters with the police and the magistrates. But an intriguing ambiguity is left by his last recorded remark: that her confession had made her interesting in his eyes. Perhaps Clarisse was acknowledging by this remembered phrase that her confession was motivated less by a desire to humor a drunk than to bolster her romantic allure. It is even more tempting to see here the work of Latouche, who may have found that Clarisse's confession had earned her a psychological profit which she would have been reluctant to recognize.

Clarisse could not resist adding a pendant to the story of her days and nights with Clémandot. Ironically, it was in the theater, which had played such an unfortunate part in their relationship, that she learned that Clémandot had betrayed to the authorities her mock confession that she was the mysterious woman at the Bancal house. It is no surprise that after she received this distressing news the performance seemed to her "tediously long." This was undoubtedly the last straw. She reacted to this ultimate theatrical setback with the fervor of the alcoholic who was so shaken by Ray Milland's performance in *The Lost Weekend* that he resolved to give up movies. Clarisse writes:

From that moment I renounced all plays, and am resolved religiously to keep my vow.

In addition to satisfying the public curiosity about her relationship with Clémandot, the *Memoirs* attempt to explain Clarisse's curious conduct in admitting and then denying that she was at the Bancals' and in finally suggesting, by her strange conduct in court, that she had firsthand knowledge of the crime. In the *Memoirs* Clarisse holds rigorously to Version Two of her testimony, namely, that she spent the fateful night at her home and that her confession of being at the scene was made in jest. She brings forward a great mass of selfless family considerations as well as personal fears to justify her departure from the truth in deposing before the prefect that she had been at the Bancals' when Fualdès was murdered.

Having leaped the hurdle of explaining Clarisse's "false" deposition, Madame Manson and her editor faced a greater challenge: how to justify her strange performance in court, which so strongly incriminated defendants of a murder of which she disclaimed all knowledge. Clarisse repeats in the *Memoirs* her earlier stories as to the attempts of Madame Pons, one of Bastide's sisters, to dissuade her from giving testimony harmful to the defendants. There is the suggestion in the book that Clarisse resented attempted threats and intercessions from friends of the defendants. In fact, she writes that at an interview before her court testimony she obtained assurances from Madame Pons of the falseness of recent reports that Jausion had asked for a dagger when he heard that Clarisse had been subpoenaed as a witness. But Clarisse's relations with Madame Pons are left in obscurity. Clarisse had told the prefect of her receipt of an anonymous note believed to have come from the defendants' supporters.

In the *Memoirs* she observes that Madame Pons had been asserted to be the author, and gratuitously adds that the assertion is "a thing not impossible." On the other hand, she refused instructions not to see Madame Pons and "saw her in no other light than that of a benefactress." Ultimately, Clarisse would have us believe, she felt so close to Madame Pons that through an intermediary she asked the woman to procure her a gun so that she could shoot Clémandot in open court and save her brother Edward, an indifferent marksman, from the danger of a duel, which he was threatening. Although disliking what she fancied to be pressure from the defendants, Clarisse acknowledges that she herself had put out feelers to the other side, and had, in fact, before the trial, requested and obtained an interview with Didier Fualdès, the son of the murdered magistrate. She found him and his conversational style charming.

Other external factors leading to her strange court performances are cited. But heavily obscured by the surface details of the *Memoirs* is an important disclosure which would link Clarisse's behavior with that of several other witnesses in the case, whom we would more readily admit to be "normal"— it would appear that Clarisse, like so many others, had decided that repeated public rumor must be right. She became convinced that if there was so much talk about a hidden woman at the scene of the murder, such a woman must have existed. Moreover, so many people believed Bastide and Jausion to be guilty, she could no longer doubt their guilt. In directly asserting their guilt or by indicating by courtroom behavior that they were guilty, she was merely giving hearsay affirmation of what a whole town knew to be true. The record of the trial at Rodez was replete with hearsay of the most remote sort, and as other witnesses were, without firsthand knowledge, piecing together the details of the crime, so Clarisse had recorded and was voicing the community's feeling as to what the jury's ultimate verdict should be. In addition, the public clearly was expecting something dramatic from Clarisse's testimony. She had to produce something for them, and if, as she claims, she knew nothing, all that was left to her was to voice and dramatize their own feelings.

But this view of the meaning of Clarisse's courtroom testimony does not emerge clearly from defenses of her conduct put forward in the *Memoirs*. Characteristically, Clarisse and her editor drew upon a large arsenal of explanations for her behavior in court, and in the end there was no explanation at all. According to Clarisse, her agreement to testify followed a particularly violent scene with her father. She notes, emphasizing her words, that *"in order to pacify him, I conceded the point once more, and promised to comply with his wishes to the fullest extent."* She appeared in the courtroom and witnessed the impaneling of the jury and the reading of the bills of indictment. A number of people around her in the courtroom "assailed" her with demands that she speak the truth, and she felt that she was being looked at with contempt by common people and avoided by "persons of respectability." Encounters with the personages of the case increased her distress. She said that she had "never suffered so acutely" as when Bastide and Jausion saluted her in court, making her apparent complicity in the crime a subject for public speculation. Matters were not made better when she spotted her foe, Clémandot, in the courtroom wearing "an air of such provoking insolence" as to reawaken her fond hopes of shooting him. These first courtroom impressions were followed by a series of interviews with different individuals seeking to exercise influence on her for a variety of reasons: her cousin Amans Rodat, who tried to talk her out of what he assumed to be an oath of silence pledged to her savior, Jausion; the president of the court, who she claimed took the unusual step of advising her that she could "tax Jausion with his presumption" in bowing to her and put such questions to him as she judged proper; a young man who approached her in the witnesses' room to advise that Madame Pons was reckoning confidently upon her; and finally, Didier Fauldès, who told her of his conviction that she was at the murder scene and begged her to identify Jausion and Bastide as assassins.

The *Memoirs* tell us that the appeal made by Didier Fualdès was persuasive. Clarisse records her reaction as follows:

A death-like shuddering overpowered me. I saw my suspicions were founded. My mind was disordered. I felt as though I had lost my senses and said, "You believe them guilty! Well! Let them perish: you shall be revenged!"

Shortly after this interview, Clarisse appeared in the court to testify. She described a mélange of emotions and impressions contributing to her disarray, but significantly places emphasis on her conviction, enforced by the words of the magistrate's son, of the guilt of the defendants:

On the one hand, the imposing solemnity of justice: the awful consequences of it exhibited by the accused: *my full conviction of their guilt:* the wild air which characterised some of their countenances: the profound silence that reigned over the immense hall: the attentive curiosity of the public, who filled it, and who expected the development of some great mystery: my knowledge of the suspicions entertained of my father: the sight of the unhappy son of him whose fate was now to be avenged: and, lastly, the image of the saviour, which stood in front and reminded me of my duty;—all these objects united, all these tumultuous ideas assailing the mind, overpowered me, and I fainted.

Despite the elaborate orchestration of the justifications laid out in the *Memoirs* for Clarisse's hysterical performance, perhaps neither Clarisse nor her editor was convinced that her conduct had been satisfactorily explained. In looking back on her testimony, Clarisse falls into her favorite pose of wonder at her own actions, the pose of "herself surprised." She writes:

... every time I peruse the details of the fatal sitting of the 22nd August, I ask myself "Are you the person who said all this. Is it possible that you could fall into the commission of such extravagan-cies?"

Interspersed in the narrative of justification for Clarisse's behavior as deponent and witness is another narrative of literary interest. It is a detective story, with Clarisse cast in the role of detective ten years before the appearance in France of the Memoirs of Vidocq and twenty-seven years before the publication of the Dupin stories of Edgar Allan Poe. The mystery is the identity of the veiled woman in hiding at the Bancals' and the denouement is Clarisse's dis-covery and conviction that the woman was Rose Pierret. It is a story that appears to be false, but this only strengthens the ground for claiming that *The Memoirs of Madame Man-son* is an early entry in the genre of mystery fiction. Since the Manson mystery story is French, it is not surprising that, in the mode of French detective stories, including the Inspec-tor Maigret series, the detection proceeds not by means of the examination and testing of physical evidence but through confrontations between the detective and various participants in the case and, finally, through the exercise of the detective's own intuition. Since Clarisse had revealed her charges against Rose Pierret at the first trial, the structure of the detective plot carries much of the fascination of the "in-verted" detective story, where the reader knows at the out-set the identity of the guilty party, and wonders how the detective will find out and just how long he will be about his business.

Clarisse indicates early in the narrative of the *Memoirs* the first clues of Rose's knowledge of the murder. On March 23, only a few days after the discovery of the body of Fualdès, Rose Pierret, in a chance meeting with Clarisse at a millinery store, described the murder in some detail and identified Bastide as one of the murderers. Clarisse confides to her readers that it did not occur to her at the time that Rose had been at the Bancal house during the tragedy. On May 18

Clarisse met Rose again at the milliner's, and Rose mentioned that "there were two persons who had not yet been seized." Clarisse was still not suspicious that Rose had any direct knowledge of the case.

We have seen that Rose also appeared in the pages of the *Memoirs* as an innocent bystander during Clémandot's amatory pursuit of Clarisse. But from time to time Rose, in conversations with Clarisse, dwelt again on the Fualdès murder. When Clarisse's brother Edward told them both that he had just seen Jausion in the street looking very pale, Rose observed that she had no desire to see him, that she pitied him and would not be at Rodez to see him executed.

Shortly after this incident, Clarisse made an interesting discovery. In a linen chest in Rose's room, she saw a large black veil "such as the Spaniards wear" and placed it on her head. When she complimented Rose on its beauty and asked her where she had bought it and how much it had cost, Rose snatched the veil away, threw it into the chest and locked it up. Although her conduct was surprising, Clarisse did not connect the incident with the Fualdès murder because she did not then know that anyone had been seen wearing a veil in the murder house.

The trail of the mystery continued to run through the world of feminine fashion. Prior to her testimony, her cousin Madame Castel warned Clarisse to admit that she had been at the Bancals'. She told Clarisse that there was a witness who would swear that on the day after the murder, the Bancals' little daughter, Madeleine, "had brought a bonnet to be made, which a lady had left her." According to Madame Castel, the bonnet was made out of the same material as one of Clarisse's gowns. A few days later, Clarisse mentioned this conversation to a gentleman in court. He recommended that she go to see Madeleine in person to examine the material of which her bonnet was made. "Perhaps," said he, "this may tend to happy discoveries."

A moment later, before she could act on this advice, she

was told by people sitting near her in court that a young woman had been summoned, and that according to report, this young woman had been in the Bancals' house. On questioning one of these court gossips, Clarisse heard that the name of Rose Pierret had just been mentioned to the president of the court "as one deeply acquainted with the whole affair." Suddenly the truth of Rose's identity as the mysterious woman dawned upon Clarisse:

In an instant, all our conversations on this subject rushed into my mind.

After several days' delay, Clarisse went to her climactic interview with little Madeleine, accompanied by the milliner who had made the meaningful bonnet. As the milliner was known to the little girl, she first presented herself alone and left Clarisse outside the door. She soon returned to Clarisse with the disappointing news that Madeleine had sent the bonnet back to her mother, who had returned her a black one instead, for her to wear in mourning for her father. Clarisse decided that a sterner interrogation was in order. She had the child brought to her, and looking at her fiercely, told her that she had just come from the court; that the child's mother had saved her own life by confessing everything; and that soldiers would be sent to fetch the child unless Clarisse obtained the truth from her. In reply to her questions, Madeleine confirmed that M. Fualdès had been killed at the Bancals' and repeated the stories that she had already told to the public. Then Clarisse promised her a crown for telling who the lady had been who was hiding in the house. Madeleine said that the lady had worn a veil, and when Clarisse drew aside hers, saying, "Look at me—am I the lady?" the girl gave the disappointing answer that she had not seen the lady's face. Nothing daunted, Clarisse dragged Madeleine off to the prefect. The prefect took a different tack, having Clarisse stand up and then asking Madeleine if the lady in hiding was of the same height. The girl produced a reply that vindicated Clarisse as detective and also, no doubt, flattered her vanity: the mysterious lady was not quite so tall as Clarisse and *"much fatter."*

The detective story breaks off here. Clarisse never clearly identifies the short, fat woman with Rose Pierret, but she does add the information that she wrote Rose a letter imploring her to disclose whatever she knew about the case. She also tells us that she received no answer.

It is probably debatable whether the narrative of the *Memoirs* shows Clarisse Manson as entirely appealing, whether in the role of flirt, witness or detective. But oddly enough, there are scattered throughout additional sidelights on her personality, which are distinctly unflattering. Armand Fouquier has referred to what he calls the "customary irrelevance" of Clarisse Manson's remarks and observations. Many examples appear in the *Memoirs*. She recalls early in the narrative that on the morning of the day following the murder, she "went into the kitchen to fetch a coffee pot." She adds that "this circumstance may not, perhaps, be unimportant." She never tells us why. Sometimes her irrelevancy appears to reflect an inappropriate human response. In recalling a communication Rose had made to her about rumors allegedly spread by the assassins that M. Fualdès had killed himself, she devotes an entire paragraph to a grammatical error Rose made in the use of "suicide" as a verb.

The *Memoirs* also show Clarisse to be vain, anxious to curry favor with every man she meets and willing to trade in dangerous gossip, particularly in her comments on Madame Pons and Rose Pierret. But much darker suggestions appear. In one scene Clarisse watches without emotion a man being conducted to a place of execution. Asked by Rose whether he is not deserving of compassion, Clarisse reveals in her answer her ready willingness both to assume that a man is guilty and to see punishment inflicted:

He is no doubt an assassin: look, he wears a red mantle. I could see with as little compunction the murderers of the unfortunate Fualdès.

Latouche appears to have inserted a passage that hardly seems designed to advance Madame Manson's cause and, in fact, may have whetted the appetites of those who continued to see the case as a political assassination. Although Clarisse was a woman given to digression, it is surprising to read a sudden expression of political opinion, apropos, it would first appear, of nothing at all:

Do not speak to me of weak people; they are more dangerous than vicious ones. We cannot guard against evils in a state of which the sovereign is devoid of energy. A weak prince is commonly the precursor of a tyrant. An example of this kind has been furnished in our times. Louis XVI prepared the revolution, of which Napoleon reaped the advantage.

This political dictum, which was introduced as if gratuitously, is then immediately tied to the Fualdès murder:

How wide a digression, you will say! It is not, perhaps, so irrelevant as it may appear; for if the death of M. Fualdès be a cruel tragedy, the preceding reign was a series of cruel tragedies, of which it would be impossible to recount the number.

The portrait of Clarisse's heart is not embellished by this passage, since it renews the impression, already made by her conversation with Rose about the prisoner being led to execution, that she could view the death of an individual human being without undue emotion. Moreover, the doubts about her compassion are now deepened. The coolness of her reaction to the prisoner's coming death could be explained by her identification of him with the murderers of the magistrate. In this second passage, however, she downplays the horror of the magistrate's murder by reference to the cruel historical setting. The relation of the Fualdès murder to a series of tragedies of the "preceding reign" also appears to pander to the readers who insisted that the Fualdès case must have a political explanation. Although the "preceding reign" quite clearly refers to the reign of Louis XVI rather than the period of the Revolution and Napoleon, and therefore the political hint thrown out by Clarisse's comments would not support the theory of a White Terror assassination, there is a suggestion that the solution of the Fualdès tragedy may lie somewhere in the French past.

Although the picture of Clarisse that emerges from the *Memoirs* is not completely unblemished, her editor, Latouche, comes off very well indeed. It must have been with real pleasure that he was able, toward the end of the narrative, to attribute the following words to Clarisse:

> I have just formed an agreeable acquaintance with a young man from Paris, who has been kind enough to visit me in prison. He has obligingly taken charge of my memoirs, and has pushed his complaisance so far as to travel eight leagues, in order to convey them to you. Without his polite interference, I should not have had the means of transmitting this voluminous epistle.

It is obvious that the Manson *Memoirs* made the best-seller lists. The British Museum Catalogue lists a sixth and seventh edition in the year of the original publication. But there is reason to doubt whether the book can be called a critical success. One of the harshest critics was none other than Clarisse Manson herself. Before the commencement of the second trial, at Albi, she accomplished the double purpose of rejecting Latouche's version of her memoirs, while at the same time attempting a solo flight into the literary heavens. She published at Albi a booklet entitled "A Plan of Her Defense Addressed to All Sensitive Hearts." As one commentator of the times noted, her plan of defense appeared much more to be a plan of attack on the editor of her popular *Memoirs*.

She wrote in her new work:

> I did not flatter myself that I could justify myself in the eyes of all the public. Moreover, there are certain individuals whose ephemeral opinion, most often based on simple appearances, matters little to me. The esteem of good people, of sensitive souls especially, will

always be precious and dear to me. There is nothing that I would not do to possess it. Knowledge of my Memoirs must have left unfavorable impressions and have increased the prejudices which are already abroad on my account. The publication of this work has grieved me. It was not my plan to publish it yet. I yielded to the ideas of others, to the most insidious arguments, and to the *flattering hope of a justification which the least delay was going to render impossible.*

Clarisse insisted that her memoirs had been prepared solely for her mother's eyes, and that this could be seen in the faulty composition, the negligence of the style and "the detailed description of acts which were quite inconsequential."

She attributed her regrettable decision to publish the *Memoirs* to two individuals who she conceded were motivated only by their sympathy for her wretched situation and by "views which were completely philanthropic." However, she did not care to hide the fact that her feelings toward the two men differed. One, apparently her cousin Amans Rodat, she referred to as a man she had always loved and respected, and whose character and principles were beyond all reproach. No such praise was lavished on her poor editor, Latouche, who no longer appears as the "kind" and "polite" young man of the *Memoirs.* Instead all her complaints were directed toward the acts and omissions of her editor. Among other things, she was annoyed that he had seen fit to include in an introduction to the *Memoirs* a summary of her early life that painted her as a woman with a romantic bent. She was unhappy that the editor had made reference to her political opinions. This showed a strange reticence in a woman who felt that she had become such a public personage as a result of the Fualdès case that she signed a subscription in behalf of the survivors of the *Medusa.* Finally, she objected to Latouche's high-flown style. She concluded:

I am not too familiar with beautiful phrases, and I shall not say, like a certain individual whose name escapes me, "Phoebe lighted the world with her silvery rays," but quite simply, "The moon was shining."

Even in literary criticism, Clarisse is unconvincing, since she seems quite capable of indulging in stylistic flourishes of her own. When she was transferred to Albi, she was asked where she would be taken for her deposition. She was told that she would be taken to the Prison of St. Cecilia. She replied that that name did not displease her, and added:

I will here be under the protection of the patroness of harmony.

Rose Pierret also attacked Latouche for lending greater publicity to Madame Manson's slanderous identification of her as the veiled woman, and Clémandot issued ungallant comments on Clarisse herself. Despite the wide circle of critical responses to the *Memoirs*, and the able rebuttals published by Latouche, Clarisse Manson was able to reserve for herself the definitive and final assault upon the integrity of the work. She delivered her attack in a characteristic manner. In her deposition at Albi, shortly before the second trial, she proceeded to change her story again. She now confessed that she *had* been at the Bancal house, but had not witnessed the crime. Still another, and more lethal account, was produced during her testimony at the second trial. When Bastide stated that he failed to recognize her, Clarisse cried, "Wretch! You don't recognize me! And yet you wanted to cut my throat." Following this *coup de théâtre,* the jury convicted most of the defendants, and Bastide, Jausion and another defendant were executed in June 1818. All charges against Clarisse Manson were dropped.

When the Fualdès case ended, after an unsuccessful prosecution of additional defendants on the basis of Clarisse's ever-expanding testimony the literary collaborators on *The Memoirs of Madame Manson,* already alienated from each other, went their separate ways. But the brief confluence of their careers takes on new significance when considered in the light of their destinies and of the judgments posterity has passed on both of them. Viewed in retrospect, Clarisse Manson and Latouche appear no longer as an oddly matched murder celebrity and editor, but as "secret sharers" of a common attraction to drama and excitement and of an ultimate reputation for unreliability.

Latouche returned to his double career in literature and journalism. As a man of literature, he never achieved the success he aspired to. His considerable output of novels is little praised. If any of them is singled out, it is *Fragoletta* (1829), whose odd hermaphroditic heroine, like Clarisse Manson, had the habit of wandering about in men's clothing. In *Fragoletta,* according to Maurice-Pierre Boyé, "one perceives with great clarity the first sound of the bell of *Mademoiselle de Maupin "*—the Gautier novel based on the career of a historic transvestite. If the main value of his fictional oeuvre is in its influence, it may be said more generally of Latouche's literary career that his principal talent was his ability to detect and encourage budding talent and to provide editorial service and judgment. Thus, though a failure as a writer, he excelled as a literary sponsor and editor, the roles in which he served Clarisse. He published at his own expense Balzac's early novel *The Chouans,* and introduced the novelist into the literary salons of Paris. Latouche is also given credit for helping to launch the literary career of George Sand. She came from the same district as Latouche and went to see him after arriving in Paris to pursue her literary career. He is said to have been extremely stern in his criticisms of the first manuscripts she showed him, and softened his views only upon reading her novel *Indiana.* Despite his harsh judgment, he earned from George Sand a more flattering portrait than Clarisse Manson has left us as a result of that earlier literary partnership. George Sand, writing of her first interview with Latouche twenty years later, recalled him as "a man of forty-five, rather heavy-set, with a face sparkling with wit, with exquisite manners and with a refined conversational style. He had a sweet and penetrating voice, a pronunciation which was aristocratic and distinct, and a manner which was at the same time caressing and mocking."

She acknowledged that Latouche remained for a long time her master in the art of writing.

The greatest debt that posterity owes Latouche is for his service as the first editor of the poetry of André Chénier, the first edition of which was published in 1819, shortly after the third trial in the Fualdès case. Ironically, in this greatest literary work of his career, as in the Manson *Memoirs* of the year before, his editorial integrity was called into question by his enemies. It has been claimed that he could not resist "collaborating" with fragmentary originals of Chénier's work.

The career of Latouche's amateur collaborator on the Manson *Memoirs,* Clarisse herself, was much less distinguished. We are told by Armand Fouquier that after her heyday in the Fualdès case, Clarisse was for a while marketed by an entrepreneur who conceived the idea of placing her on show (like Lola Montez in the Max Ophuls film) at the counter of a café of the Palais Royal, and that she also made further sales of memoirs. Afterward, according to Fouquier's cryptic account, Clarisse fell into obscurity, "accorded a pension of 1000 francs by Count Decazes in compensation for her services."

We hear nothing of any later literary efforts on her part. Perhaps the vein of imagination that she had displayed during the trial had been exhausted. However, modern study of the documents of the trial by the distinguished police criminologist Dr. Edmond Locard suggests that Clarisse must be credited posthumously with some additional literary creations. In his work *Le Magistrat Assassiné (Affaire Fualdès),* published in France in 1954, Dr. Locard states that his analysis of the handwriting of one of the threatening letters Clarisse claimed to have received from those who wanted her to remain silent shows that the letter was forged by Clarisse. If Locard's conclusions are correct, then Clarisse's compulsion to create fiction and to put her myths into writing may have contributed to what he and other modern commentators regard as a miscarriage of justice in the Fualdès case.

CHAPTER TEN

The Jackal and I,
or How to Do Research in London

I was impressed with the research that the Jackal did in London. When the criminal genius of *The Day of the Jackal* had need of an English identity, he moved efficiently through the death records of Somerset House and even was aided by an inscription on a London gravestone. It was therefore only human for me to suppose that when my researches for a historical article required me to establish the date and circumstances of the death of a composer in seventeenth-century London, I could follow in the Jackal's footsteps.

I thought that the logical place to begin my detective work was the Reading Room of the British Museum. I obtained a letter of recommendation from a college professor and wrote to the British Museum Library requesting admission to the Reading Room during my trip to London planned for a few months off. It was gratifying to receive very promptly a response from the library enclosing an official form granting my request, which could be exchanged at the museum for an admission ticket at any time during the next six months. The beginning was promising. The Jackal himself could not have done better.

When I arrived in London I waited for the jet lag to recede slightly, then rushed to the British Museum. At a police barrier that had been set up on the front steps, I dutifully presented my briefcase for inspection. Once inside the door, I made straight for the guards at the entrance to the Reading Room. Flashing my official permission, I explained that I had been granted by mail the right to obtain a reader's ticket.

"That seems rather obvious," said one of the guards, glancing contemptuously at my correspondence and dismissing me with a wave in the direction of the Ticket Room. I wasn't sure that my reception had been friendly, but at least my credentials appeared to be in order.

At the Ticket Room, I was duly registered and given two tickets—one to the Reading Room and one to the Manuscript Division—plus a brochure containing closely printed instructions on use of the library. The instructions somewhat exceeded in length the United Nations Charter, and in sections would have benefited by the charter's multilingual versions.

I advanced to the Reading Room, where I digested the library regulations. I was a bit concerned by the warning that books took at least an hour and a half to be delivered, but a quick survey of the shelves of general reference material in the vast Reading Room Rotunda comforted me with the assurance that I would keep busy.

Murmuring the principal library regulations in a rhythmical cadence in the hope of committing them to memory, I set out to hunt for the card index so that I could order my first books. I found that there was no card index. Instead there were circular shelves of bound index volumes, which also served as a protective wall for the library staff. Courageously slipping through one of the gaps in the wall, which had been left unattended, and trying not to listen to the intimate library gossip, I located my index volume.

Inside, along the left margin of each page, in alphabetical order, were pasted printed book descriptions, of the sort that in humbler climes appear on index cards. Bound index volumes do have certain obvious advantages. You have the literary pleasure, from the very moment you start your library work, of hugging a book to your bosom (in all but the most dramatic cases, the book would be much larger than the bosom). Also, you may move the book wherever you like along the circumference of the hedge of shelves, for solitary perusal, and do not have to hover communally over index drawers in the company of all sorts of scholars you don't care to meet. That, I assume, must be the English view of things.

Of course, there are disadvantages. For example, some author may have the lack of foresight to bear a name or choose a title for which there simply will be no space in the alphabetical sequence of the left-hand index column. But for this problem the canny English have a solution. There is sometimes room along the right margin for supplemental insertions of new titles (say, those since 1850), and if these concessions to modernity cannot be made in strict alphabetical order, the new insertions generally will have the same first letter as the left-hand entries and will be sure to whet the appetite for rapid page-turning. Nevertheless, I think that if I were an aspiring English author, I would first hunt for gaps in the alphabetical listings of the British Museum and then select a pseudonym accordingly. I would also keep my titles short.

After assembling data from the index volume, I confidently ordered my first books. When close to three hours went by without a delivery, I thought I would borrow a technique from the obstetricians and attempt to "induce" delivery. I approached the order desk and engaged the attention of the order clerk, a girl apparently on the verge of attaining her twelfth birthday. She told me that the delivery time tended to lengthen out around the lunch hour, which had just passed, but that since three hours had gone by, my orders should be traced. I thanked her, and asked her how long it would take her to trace the books. She told me with a shocked expression that the Order Department did not *trace* orders, but that I must address myself to the Inquiries Desk.

At the Inquiries Desk, one of the supervisors listened apathetically and held up a card containing perhaps fifty multidigit code numbers.

"Do you remember whether your call numbers are on this list?" he asked. "If so, you're in for a long wait because your books are in another building."

Confessing the lack of a photographic memory, I shrugged at the card and resigned myself to calling again the next day. And I did, and many days after that. Finally one of my books arrived and I read it with the sharpened interest that comes from a long quest. None of my other books turned up, but in each case I received instead a Message.

Message One said: "Book is at bindery. Inquire at Inquiry Desk." At the desk my supervisor with the call-number flash card explained: "A book can be recalled from the bindery in about a week in case of emergency. Is it an emergency?" It was hard to think that the death of a composer, if it was ever an emergency, could continue to be so for three hundred years. I retired ingloriously.

It was about this time that I was beginning to wonder how my fellow scholars in the Reading Room would ever complete their studies. As I looked around the rotunda, many of the researchers appeared quite young. But I considered the possibility that the library held some Shangri-la charm, and that when, after arduous periods of waiting and hoping, the readers went out into Great Russell Street, they would age by centuries and crumble into dust.

Message Eight was the most hopeful: "Your book is posted on the Green Board."

I rushed enthusiastically to the Inquiries Desk. Breathlessly I murmured, "Take me to the Green Board. My book is posted there."

My old antagonist, the inquiry supervisor, shook his head as he looked over my message slip, and said, "You don't understand. Your book has been lost. The Green Board is the place where we list officially lost books."

It was shortly afterward that I decided to give up the Reading Room and to surrender my tickets, a formality required of departing students, which I suppose is the scholarly equivalent of broken sword or torn epaulet. As I went down the steps of the museum, no longer feeling the equal of the Jackal, I noticed the police barrier again and the continuing search of briefcases. The police were obviously looking for bombs, but I was not sure now whether they were concerned about the IRA or hostile scholars.

In view of the heavy intellectual matter that has preceded, I shall pause for an entr'acte in which I will discourse on the problems that scholars (as well as residents, for that matter) are presented by duplication of English street names.

Having had enough of libraries for a while, I decided to visit a London bookshop that I thought might have some books of interest to me in connection with my researches. A book dealers' directory told me it was on James Street. Unfortunately, there is more than one James Street in London (not to mention St. James streets). By process of elimination, I determined that *my* James Street must be in Covent Garden, but at the street number listed in the directory I found no bookstore, but instead a fruit warehouse. Having gained in tenacity by dint of my British Museum experiences, I called the dealer's telephone number from a nearby kiosk, and learned that I had indeed found the right place and that the dealer was located in the warehouse building four floors above the apples. The book dealer was surprised that I had not seen his sign.

I made an appointment and returned to the warehouse at the hour fixed. The dealer was right. His name did appear on the door. The "sign" was a one-inch-by-two-inch calling card, which was pasted on the doorframe. I rang the bell, with no response, but a girl leaned out a high window and told me that the proprietor was probably on his way back from the pub. This proved to be the first completely accurate piece of information I had received in the course of my researches, and the book dealer soon appeared to lead me through a low metal door built to accommodate Snow White's friends, past hundreds of cartons of apples giving off a powerful perfume, and up into the literary heaven on the fourth floor. I know that it is an illusion, but the odor of apples still seems to cling to my research files.

Confusing English street names can not only stymie a scholar, but can further a murder scheme. On January 20, 1931, William Herbert Wallace, a Liverpool insurance agent, left his home to call upon a prospective client, named R. M. Qualtrough, who had made the appointment by telephone the evening before. Qualtrough had given his address as 25 Menlove Gardens East. Mr. Wallace searched without success for Menlove Gardens East, though he discovered Menlove Gardens North, South and West. He then returned home to find that in his absence his wife had been brutally murdered. That was Wallace's story, but the police and the trial jury thought that Wallace had murdered his wife before he left home and had invented both Mr. Qualtrough and the elusive address.

My experiences with confusing street names are, of course, pale by comparison with Mr. Wallace's. But on another occasion, I was drenched to the skin while trying to distinguish among Kensington Gardens, Kensington Terrace, Kensington Gate and Kensington Mews. If you are not more expert on London streets than I, I would suggest you bring an umbrella.

Leaving the world of books, I plunged into London's burial registers, will indexes and court records. My path led me from the Guildhall Library to the County Hall and the Middlesex Record Office. The complexity of my search was partially explained by the stubborn refusal of the ancient City of London to merge its government or archives with those of the surrounding metropolis. But I was soon convinced that I had become the victim of the Londoner's innate joy in duplication and fragmentation for their own sake.

My search finally narrowed to the records of the Royal

Court of the King's Bench, which were maintained, I was told, in the Public Record Office, Chancery Lane. At the archway to the Record Office, I was challenged by a uniformed guardian of his nation's statistics and told to apply upstairs for a temporary visitor's pass. When I returned with the pass, it became clear that I was only on the first leg of a documentary scavenger's hunt. I was directed by the guard to an entrance "under the clock" and up another staircase to the inquiry room. There, among a hopeless throng resembling the denizens of the waiting room of Menotti's Consul, I obtained application form and regulations for another in my growing collection of reader's tickets.

"Great," I said to the receptionist who faced me across a table. "I'll fill out the form here."

"I don't think that will be possible, sir," I was told. "Foreigners must present a letter of recommendation from an English lawyer."

When I indicated a reluctance to disturb my legal colleagues in London, I was told that a letter from the American embassy would do. As I pondered the long journey to Grosvenor Square, the receptionist consoled me by advising that records could not be delivered to me that day anyway since the crepuscular hour of 3 P.M. had already arrived. He stretched a point by permitting me an illegal entry into the reading room, where I asked the curator for the call number for King's Bench court records.

Full of the sense that I was drawing close to the quarry, I obtained a laconic note from a representative of the American ambassador and returned to the Public Record Office the next morning. At first, things went with a deceptive smoothness. Up the stairs; temporary visitor's permit; to the clock; up a second stairway; to the inquiry room; admission ticket at last.

In the reading room I filled out my document order with a flourish, forearmed as I was with the call number. I handed it to the curator, reminding him in my best transoceanic manner of yesterday's conversation. However, he had distinctly cooled overnight.

"Give the slip to the lady at the counter," he said.

"There is no lady at the counter," was my factual reply.

"Then put it in the slot," he said, pointing to a pigeonhole right before him.

I complied, and the curator immediately withdrew the slip from the pigeonhole and read it.

"You can't have the record today," he told me.

"Why not?" I asked with sinking hopes.

"It's kept at the assize office outside London. It will take a week to bring it here."

Instead of asking why he hadn't given me this news the day before, I replied cheerfully, "That's all right; I will be in London one more week. I'll be back Monday."

Then the curator played his trump. "No, you won't. Next week we're closed for inventory."

I decided on the spot to conclude my London researches. When I compared my dismal fate with the Jackal's triumphant fact-finding, I began to feel that *The Day of the Jackal* was not a crime novel, as I had originally thought—it was science fiction.

My story, in one particular, has a happy ending. When I returned home, I found a copy of the Green Board book at the Cleveland Public Library, where it was delivered to me about five minutes after I ordered it.

The lesson to be drawn from my experiences is clear. If you plan to do research in London, you should have one of two assets going for you: You should be either a saint or extremely long-lived. It would be preferable if you could be both.